American Singers

American Singers

Whitney Balliett

NEW YORK   OXFORD UNIVERSITY PRESS   1979

Library of Congress Cataloging in Publication Data

Balliett, Whitney.
    American singers.

    "A group of portraits of leading American popular
and jazz singers."
    1. Singers—United States—Biography.
    2. Jazz musicians—United States—Biography.
ML400.B25   784'.092'2   [B]   78-21545
ISBN 0-19-502524-5

"Just a Singer" appeared in *New York Notes* (Houghton Mifflin);
"It's Detestable When You Live It" and "The Human Sound" in
Ecstasy at the Onion (Bobbs-Merrill); and "A Quality That Lets You
In," "Absolutely Pure" ("Hanging Out with Blossom Dearie"), and
"A Queenly Aura" in *Alec Wilder and His Friends* (Houghton
Mifflin). The rest of the chapters were first printed in *The New
Yorker Magazine*. All the material is now in somewhat different form.

Printed in the United States of America

For Teddi King

Note

Why this group of portraits was put together and what it is about is spelled out in the opening of the first chapter. *American Singers* is certainly not comprehensive, nor is it a history or a study of American non-classical singing. The singers included are here because they are first-rate and because they were available, as other first-rate singers were not. The book was written during the past decade as an act of homage to a highly gifted and unaccountably neglected group of American artists.

New York
October 1978   W. B.

Contents

American Singers

American Singers

Teddi King
Mary Mayo
Barbara Lea

A certifiable body of classic American songs now exists, and we need an elegant and accurate phrase to describe them. These songs, variously and disconcertingly known as "pop songs," "popular songs," "counter songs," "novelty tunes," or "show tunes," have been composed during the past seventy years for the stage, the movies, and Tin Pan Alley by the likes of Jerome Kern, Irving Berlin, George Gershwin, Cole Porter, Richard Rodgers, Fats Waller, Harold Arlen, Duke Ellington, Willard Robison, Vincent Youmans, Hoagy Carmichael, Alec Wilder, Ann Ronell, Vernon Duke, and Stephen Sondheim. Modern American songs are not lieder. Their harmonies, melodies, rhythms, and forms are altogether different, as are their emotional impetus and effect. They are not art songs—a term that smacks of chapbooks and colloquiums. And they are not just popular songs or non-academic songs or jazz songs or cabaret songs or supper-club songs or theatre songs or movie songs. The belated recognition that they are not ephemeral, that they are the work of melodists directly descended from Tchaikovsky and Puccini and Rachmaninoff, has been brought about by many things, among them Alec Wilder's judicious and witty work of classification and criticism, *American Popular Song;** the Wilder-organized radio shows given over to performances of the best American songs by the best American singers; Mabel Mercer's continued reign as the queen of American singers; the brilliant recitals given at Town Hall and the Ninety-second Street "Y" in New York in the early seventies by the late Johnny Mercer; Bobby Short's sempiternal engagement at the Café Carlyle; and the increasingly frequent appearances by Anita Ellis, Barbara Lea, Marlene VerPlanck, Mary Mayo, Sylvia Syms, Helen Merrill, Johnny Hartman, Helen Humes, Tony Bennett, Nancy Harrow, David Allyn, Blossom Dearie, Hugh Shannon, Mark Murphy, Margaret Whiting, Matt Dennis, Jackie Cain, Dick Haymes, Mel Tormé, Peggy Lee, and Maxine Sullivan.

The singers who have been carrying forward this movement have made the beauty and ingenuity of American songs clear. They are the first to join the two principal strains in American singing: the "popular" kind (pioneered largely by Gene Austin and Ruth Etting and Bing Crosby and traceable to European light-classical music) and jazz singing (pioneered largely by Ethel Waters and Louis Armstrong and Billie Holiday and traceable to blues and gospel and instrumental music). They possess qualities that few of their forebears had forty years ago, when the first sizable wave of "popular" singers appeared. Those singers worked chiefly with the big bands, and were wholly functional. They were intuitive and homemade, pushing their songs along before them, and praying that they would stay on pitch and finish in the same bar as their accompanists. Most big-band fans considered them unnecessary and boring—interludes to be tolerated until the next "instrumental," with its complement of solos. They were obliged to sing dread-

---

* *American Popular Song* by Alec Wilder (New York: Oxford University Press, 1972).

ful, of-the-moment material, and to sit on camp chairs at the front of the bandstand throughout the evening. Primitive sound systems, or even the band, made them inaudible to themselves and to those in the audience who *did* want to hear them. Their descendants are more fortunate, and are far better equipped. They are excellent musicians who can sing a song exactly as written (many have had classical training) and then, using their knowledge of Mildred Bailey and Billie Holiday and Mabel Mercer, improvise or enlarge on it. They are at once better schooled and more inventive than their predecessors. They are masters of diction, timing, intonation, and melody. Most are middle-aged, and came up during the last days of the big bands. Surviving the forties, they foundered on rock in the fifties, although a small number worked in studios and in the hotels of Las Vegas and Miami. The dilution of rock and the disappearance of the 10 per cent federal entertainment tax have helped their renaissance, but the few big bands left rarely hire singers of their sort, and neither does television. Hospitable night clubs have appeared around the country, but even these are prone to fads or poor judgment. So it is always a joyous occasion when the new singers land jobs.

Three of the most gifted and tenacious of the new singers have been Mary Mayo, Barbara Lea, and the late Teddi King. Teddi King died in November of 1977. She suffered from a debilitating disease, but few knew of her illness, and she never allowed it to affect her demeanor or her singing. She was a miniature person. Her hands and feet were tiny, and her small, pretty face was dominated by lustrous eyes. She was barely five feet tall, but her voice was large and relaxed. When she performed, she invariably wore a hat, which was like adding a mansard roof to a bungalow. She had a rich contralto and a wide vibrato, and a peaceful, spacious way of phrasing. She never hurried a note, even at fast tempos, and she gave each song a serenity that carried it through the noisiest room. The particulars of her style were less important than the harmonious wholes she made of her songs. Traces of Lee Wiley and Mildred Bailey showed up, but her work was her own. She loved to talk, and she had a Boston accent and a pealing, old-fashioned laugh. She lived in a big apartment on the Upper West Side with her husband, Josh Gerber, who is shy and genial, and is an expert society-band drummer. She had a quick, dancing, half-moon smile, and it lit up the rare pauses between her sentences. She talked about herself one afternoon in New York not long before she died:

"Josh and I were married in 1949, and by then I was *the* lady singer in Boston. I worked with Nat Pierce's band, and I was on all three of the local musical television shows. George Wein opened his first Storyville Club, in the Buckminster Hotel, and I got to know him and Charlie Bourgeois. Charlie started waving my banner around. Storyville moved to a bigger place, in the Copley Square Hotel, and George Shearing came in with his quintet. I sang for him, and he said my sound fitted the sound of the quintet. I went with him for two years, beginning in the fall of 1952, and the whole association was a joy. Then I went out on my own, and worked places like Mr. Kelly's, in Chicago, and the Rendezvous, in Philadelphia. John Carradine was in the show at the Rendezvous, and one night he sat out front and stared at me, and when I finished he said, 'I want to thank you for not shouting at us.' Those were musically happy years, but they ended when George Wein became too busy to handle me, and I took on a New York manager. He didn't know the cloth I was made of. He didn't know the subtleties of my work. All he knew was Las Vegas. So I had an act written and sequinned gowns made, and I went to Vegas. I signed a contract with RCA Victor, and I had a couple of singles that did very well. I worked the big rooms and was on network TV, and the public became aware of my name. But it wasn't me. I was doing pop pap, and I was in musical despair. I didn't have my lovely jazz music and the freedom it gives. Elvis Presley got bigger and bigger, and rock arrived, and I got very depressed and thought of quitting the business. Josh and I had kept a little apartment in Boston, and we went back to it. George Wein had just moved to New York, and he told us we should, too, so we did. I opened the Playboy Club in New York and stayed there off and on through the sixties.

"I took a job on Nantucket the summer of 1970. The first day I went to the beach, I started feeling strange. I could barely maneuver, and I got a rash on my arms. I was in and out of the hospital on Nantucket all summer, but no one could find out what was wrong until I went to the Pratt Clinic, in Boston, where they diagnosed what I had as systemic lupus erythematosus. It attacks women more often than men, and it goes after the connective tissue. Flannery O'Connor eventually died of it. You take cortisone. It makes you very susceptible to infection, so you can't get too fatigued, and you have to stay out of the sun. I was bedridden quite a while, and my main concern was whether I'd be able to sing again. Then I started to mend, and in 1971 I worked at the Columns, in West Dennis, on Cape Cod, with Dave McKenna. They gave me a room upstairs, and the whole thing was a terrific tonic. Dave is one of the great accompanists. Bobby Hackett, who had just moved to the Cape, would sit in, and *he* was one of the great accompanists, too. I've been working where I could since then—at festivals and on Alec Wilder's program and for six weeks at the Café Carlyle last winter.

"I think my illness changed the emphasis in my singing. I've always been enamored of sound, but I was afraid I might not have the voice I'd had, and I began concentrating on lyrics. That, and I fell under the influence of Mabel Mercer, who is my goddess now. I'd never dwelt on lyrics: I sang them and that was all. But I began watching Mabel, to see how she touched people, and I discovered it was the way she put the lyrics first. Her lyrics are her magic. Then she told me that, no matter how beautiful its melody, she selects a new song only after she has gone over its lyrics to see if they have any meaning for her. When I sing, I'm in a little shell. I feel as if I'm reciting a poem. If there is a person in the lyrics—in 'It Never Entered My Mind' or 'Little

Girl Blue' or 'I'm in the Market for You'—I become that person. The lyrics direct my choice of notes. They take over, and I can just open my mouth and the sound follows. So I don't think ahead in my phrasing, and every time I do a song it comes out slightly differently. My singing is also influenced by the external things of the moment, like the room or the people or the accompanist. A good accompanist breathes with you. An inferior one forces you back into yourself.

"My mother had a glorious natural voice, and she and my father, who was a song-and-dance man in vaudeville, were always singing and listening to music on the radio. I was born Theodora, and I'm a Bostonian, purebred. My mother lost three other children, so I became an only child. She has never changed—shy and sweet and childlike. She leaned heavily on my father for suggestions and interest, and then followed through on her own. He died about a year ago, but she's kept their big old apartment in Revere. My dad was self-educated and well read, and he could have gone into anything. He was handsome and had a little mustache, and he had such presence that when my parents gave a party everyone sat and waited in the living room—it was as if they were waiting for Godot—until my father came in. Then the party started. When vaudeville gave out, he got into a printing-and-publishing firm and became a proof-reader. My talent surfaced when I was four and sang 'Am I Blue?' in a great deep voice. I took classical piano for a year in the sixth grade, and since I'm a very disciplined person, I went on by myself, using whatever piano books the teacher had given me. It still relaxes me to play Bach and Debussy. Then we moved to Malden, and I finished school there. I was in the glee club, but I was more interested in acting than in singing, and I joined the dramatic club in high school. I minded not being able to afford going to college, but the Boston school system was marvellous then, and a high-school diploma was the equivalent of at least a year of college. And I knew that it's not impossible to absorb learning by yourself if you have a mind to. I went into a typing-and-shorthand job after school, but my head was in the arts, and I tried out for a repertory company called the Tributary Theatre of Boston. It was in the New England Mutual Hall, and it played Shakespeare and O'Casey and light American comedy. I did a couple of readings for them, using a lot of accents—they liked it, and I loved doing it, because accents have always seemed to me to reveal the inner cadence of a country. They also discovered I sang, which I'd been doing right along on the side, so they gave me the role of a singing mermaid in a musical *Peter Pan*. I wasn't listed in the program, but Elliot Norton, the Boston critic, wrote in glowing terms about the young lady who played the mermaid and sang, and that triggered something in me: maybe I should think more seriously about singing. I never missed a show at the R.K.O. I'd sit in the front row with my lunch to see Sinatra and Helen Forrest and Helen O'Connell and Jo Stafford. When the R.K.O. had a Dinah Shore sing-alike contest, I entered it and beat out five hundred girls. My singing career began immediately. Winning night, two young gentlemen came backstage and said, 'We caught the show and wonder if you would be interested in singing with a friend who's starting a band.' The friend was George Graham, and he'd just come off Georgie Auld's band. He had a complement of the best musicians in town, and I joined for five dollars a night. They were at the Ritz Ballroom, on Huntington Avenue near Symphony Hall, and I was there for several months. I suppose I sounded like Billie Holiday, because she had influenced me a great deal. Then I took a weekend job with Jack Edwards at the Coral Gables Ballroom in Weymouth, on the South Shore. They were grooming him to be another Vaughn Monroe, and we had a lot of radio remotes. I was paid thirty-five dollars, so I quit my day job as a typist at the Boston Navy Yard. A family club called Cappy's, in Easton, Massachusetts, near Brockton, hired me next. Josh was the drummer, and I got to know him driving back and forth to Boston. This was 1946, and for the next three years I sang around Boston. I also studied voice with Mrs. Chester MacDonald, who had taught at the New England Conservatory. She said I had natural voice placement, and within six months I was singing lyric and coloratura things. She was heartbroken when I left her after a year. I studied a little jazz piano, too, which helped me with chords and changes, with dominant sevenths and flatted fifths. I feel best now when I'm working. The rest of the time, I take it easy and let the silly, petty things roll off my back."

Mary Mayo has an extraordinary range. She has said, "My voice runs from low A below middle C to A-flat above high C. I used to be able to go to C above high C, but it's not something you ever need." She can be compared to Sarah Vaughan, but Vaughan's voice is heavier and less subtle. Her lowest register is cavernous but somewhat harsh, her middle tones are three deep, and her high range is rather piping. Mary Mayo's instrument is of a piece from top to bottom. Her highest register is liquid and effortless, and it pours into her serene middle range. Her lowest register is a silken evening voice. She does not hit her notes dead center but favors the area just a hair above, which gives her singing a light, suspended quality. Of the singers of her generation, she is the most limpid and graceful. Her diction, like Teddi King's and Barbara Lea's, is faultless; she sets each word before the listener. She is of average height, and she has broad shoulders and a heart-shaped face. Her coloring and manner reflect her singing: platinum-blond hair, very white skin, and a beacon smile. She moves little when she performs, but she takes on an intense, almost beseeching look, which, underlined by her broad dynamics, becomes inescapable in a song like "Molly Malone." She is married to Al Ham, an independent record producer, and they have a daughter, Lorri, who is studying acting and who also sings. Mary Mayo lives in a light-filled apartment high over Morningside Park. It is a suitable aerie for her voice. She smiles a great deal when she talks, and her speech is tinted with a Piedmont accent:

"My father, Franklin Riker, was born in Burlington, Vermont, and he came to New York in 1888, when he was twelve. Someone heard him sing in a choir up there and recommended that he move to the city. He lived in Brooklyn with an aunt and was a boy-soprano soloist at Old Trinity Church, downtown. He eventually became a *helden-tenor*, and he sang at the Met when Caruso was there. He studied in Europe with Jean de Reszke, Cotogni, and Stahlschmidt. He returned to America just before the First World War, prepared for *Tristan* and *Siegfried*, but Wagner had been put away for the duration. After the war, he did sing Wagner, in English, and then he went into teaching. My father was a tender, kind man. He had very blue eyes, and his hair was white when he was thirty. He was robust and had pink cheeks, and his hands were always warm. My mother's name was Lois Long, and she was born in Statesville, North Carolina. She's ninety-three, but she's still a pixie and full of spunk. She used to play softball and ride sidesaddle. She and my father met in New York. She had had an early, unhappy marriage, and had a daughter, and was studying at the Master School of Music. My father heard her sing in church. She was a lyric coloratura, but he thought she could be a dramatic soprano. He told her, 'You're not using the best part of your voice.' She was furious, but eventually he convinced her, and she became a Flagstad singer, a Traubel singer. Her voice had a certain opulence and was a perfect instrument. There were no breaks in it, and she never had to make adjustments in going up and down the scale. She'd take a high F or G, and it would envelop you. It came at you, and it was globular. I've never heard that sound anywhere else except in Farrell and early Tebaldi. Once after I had sung for her, she said, 'You've got to realize, my darling, that you're just a silver bell.'

"When I came along, my mother went home to Statesville. I was born just after midnight. She had been playing bridge and listening to Galli-Curci records. There always seemed to be at least a half-dozen adults around when I was growing up. They made you insecure and yet you tended to lean on them. We moved to Philadelphia when I was two, and not long after that my father was offered a job at the Cornish School, in Seattle. We lived in the Hotel Sorrento there, and I became addicted to hotels. I was the only child in the hotel, and one Christmas I got sixty-five dolls. One had white silk hair pulled back in a bun and was several feet tall. Then we moved to San Francisco, to another residential hotel, and I learned to love foghorns and the sea. The Met touring company was looking for a second lead to Lily Pons, and my mother auditioned twice and got the job. But something went wrong within my family back in Statesville—some sort of a financial reversal—and Mother had to decide between the job with the Met company and going home, and of course she went home. I'd visited Statesville every summer and Christmas since we'd moved to the Coast, so I knew what it was like, but I missed the sea and the fog so much that I cried for a year.

"I finished high school in Statesville, and did two years of college—one at Mitchell College, at home, and one at Peace College, in Raleigh. When I was eighteen, I came up to Juilliard to study classical singing. I had won the G. Schirmer Award for high musical attainment. I had also won a prize in a singing contest sponsored by the Norge refrigerator people when I was fourteen. The song was 'Ah! Sweet Mystery of Life.' I didn't study singing until after I was fifteen, because my father felt that children sing naturally and correctly, and I'd always had a very easy voice. I studied with my father my first year of college, and continued those studies at Juilliard. But we had a lot of popular music around the house. My father admired Jerome Kern very much, and even knew him, and my grandmother was a Gene Autry fan and was invariably willing to listen when I learned the latest song. So I was ready for what I heard when I got to New York—Woody Herman and Dizzy Gillespie and Coleman Hawkins. Hawkins' 'How Deep Is the Ocean?' and 'Body and Soul' sent me on my way. I stayed at Juilliard a year, and in 1946 I won an Arthur Godfrey talent show and worked for him briefly. I spent a summer on the Normandie Roof of the Mount Royal Hotel, in Montreal. They wanted a singer who looked and sang like a lady, and I was paid fifty dollars a week. They gave me room and board, and on Sundays, when I was off, I sat in the room and read magazines and ate bonbons. In the fall, I was with Frankie Carle for three weeks, and then, through a singer named Elise Bretton, whom I met in a choral group, I went with Tex Beneke and the Glenn Miller Orchestra. I became a Moonlight Serenader, and was also given solos. Al Ham played bass in the band and wrote for it, and we fell in love. In Olympia, Washington, we were married secretly, because people in the band weren't supposed to be married to each other, but Walter Winchell broke the news twelve days later. Tex gave us his blessing anyway. After a few months, Al and I came in off the road and starved for a while in New York. We did some club dates and I got some commercials. Then Johnny Mercer heard a test recording of 'Blue Moon' that I had made, and I was signed by Capitol Records. That helped me get a job on the Frank Sinatra show. Someone told me he'd said, 'I don't like girl singers, but I like that one.' It was a hard time for him, emotionally and in his career. He was chasing Ava Gardner, and he was out of fashion as a singer. He was also a perfectionist. He'd check my camera shots, he'd check my hair, and we'd have long runthroughs. But nothing went right. Frank opened the show with the verse of 'Bewitched,' and the mike was dead. The stagehands took a long time getting the curtains right, and someone dropped a sandbag that just missed Frank. We had a new director each week. By the fourth week, I was dropped. But the job helped, and I worked steadily until 1956, when Lorri was born, and for ten years I went to mothering. I'm a categorized person, and I couldn't sing and mother at the same time. Anyway, everything has happened to me by luck. I have absolutely no drive. In the sixties, I started in at the studios again, doing commercials and such, and I worked for Al, too. I sang the title song he wrote on the soundtrack of *Harlow*. Last March, I spent two weeks at Michael's Pub. That was the first New York club date I'd had in twenty-five years, and I loved it and am ready for more.

"My specialty at Juilliard was French art songs. I had grown up with Galli-Curci and Lawrence Tibbett and Paul Robeson. If I had studied more, I would have been a lyrico-spinto, which is a kind of wedding of Tebaldi and Sills. But I ended up a lyric coloratura. I have always loved the freeness and velvetiness and roundness of the great classical voice. I would like to have those qualities, and I would also like to have the sound Joe Venuti got on his violin, and the sounds of Johnny Hodges and Benny Carter and Ben Webster. I missed Billie Holiday and Mildred Bailey, but I've admired Nat Cole—the Cole of the Trio—and Jo Stafford and Margaret Whiting and Ella Fitzgerald and Peggy Lee and certain things about Doris Day. Margaret Whiting is a terrific example of how to pronounce words. The way she sings 'you're' is so clear. It's not 'your' and not 'you are' but 'you're.' My father believed that you should warm up like a pitcher before you sing, that you shouldn't perform without reaching a certain 'intensity of mood.' To gain this, you should stand very quietly, with a straight back, and sing a soft vowel sound, sustain it, and change the vowel when you move up a tone. You do this for half an hour, eventually locking yourself into the general vocal area you'll be working in that day. When I sing, I feel whatever the song is saying. The lyrics light up the melody—give the melody a tongue. Most melodies are dumb before they have words. I wish to get into the person's head—the listener's head. I don't sing at people, I sing *to* them. Even in a theatre, I pick out one face and sing to it. If I have rehearsed enough, everything becomes spontaneous, and I don't need to worry about melody, or about anything. It isn't fair to the audience to be concerned whether your earring is going to get tangled in your hair or your heel is going to get caught in the hem of your gown. My earlier singing was pretty and melodramatic, but now I'm giving a great deal more of *me*. I'm a different singer now from what I was seven or ten years ago. I've started improvising. You find yourself eventually. I remember one of the early reviews I got. It said something to the effect that I was a pleasant enough singer but, alas, a not too exciting one. Things like that stay in your head—particularly when they're right. I'm anything but an exhibitionist, but I'm always aware that, whether I like it or not, when I stand there singing I'm naked."

Barbara Lea is a singers' singer. She has no appreciable style, because style implies self, and when she sings she puts her ego to one side and attempts to make each song exactly what its composer and lyricist intended. She has a deep, dry, forceful voice; her tones resonate. She also has an even vibrato, great rhythmic agility, sharp dynamics, and voice timbres that move from soft to sandpaper. One immediately senses the bell of deliberation she moves under. Offstage, she has a damn-the-torpedoes manner, and she always seems slightly incredulous. Her face is square and handsome, and her chin determined. Her eyes slope at the corners, and her smile moves carefully from right to left. Her hair is reddish and short. She lives on West Fifty-fifth Street, not far from the old Fifty-fifth Street Playhouse, above which another determined singer, Sylvia Syms, once lived. Barbara Lea has a canny ear, and she likes to talk about singers and singing:

"Billie Holiday couldn't sing a song without embellishments. What she did, especially in the early days, was terribly honest and direct. She flattened out the melody of her songs. She could swing incredibly. Sweet-and-sour, dill pickles, strong, cutting—she was an absolute. She sprang full grown from the head of Jove. Mabel Mercer ushered in a new era of singing. She ushered in the era of paying attention to each word. Before, sad was sad and happy happy, and they were always the same. She became terrifically specific with lyrics. She is a singing actress, as was Ethel Waters, who was outside the general run of singers. Frank Sinatra was the first big singer who took great care with his phrasing. He was a *purposeful* singer. He paid attention.

There is a lot of shtick in Sarah Vaughan. She doesn't value songs. But she has a fine voice and a fine ear. When Mel Tormé sings straight, he sings beautifully. His tone is second to no one's. I wish he didn't have to be a star. I wish he could be a nobody, he's so talented. Bobby Short structures a song beautifully. He gives it such a dramatic lift. When he's got it together, his movements are marvellous—eyes, face, shoulders. And he'll break out those hands. He's not self-indulgent.

"Nor have I ever been. I was born in Detroit, and we moved out to Melvindale, which is near Dearborn, when I was very little. We were always singing and making music around my home. I grew up assuming everyone could sing and play instruments. My brother, who sang, tap-danced, and played harmonica, kept winning amateur contests. It was the age of amateur nights. People still entertained themselves, and it was still possible to be a Hollywood star. I was born Barbara LeCocq, which was changed to Leacock when I was four or five. I started using Lea when I made my first recordings, in the early fifties, and I've also had three married names. My father was an assistant attorney general in Michigan. He could be a brilliant, charming, sparkling man, and other times he could be critical and picky and putting-down. He probably should have been a classical clarinettist. He played in the pit band for Al Jolson's *Sinbad* after the First World War, and he studied with the first clarinettist of the New York Philharmonic. But, with his strict background, it was unthinkable to go into music. My mother is intelligent and fun, and everybody loves her. She wasn't around a lot when I was little. She worked, and my grandmother took care of me. But she's very motherly, my mother. There were hard times when we lived in Melvindale, even though we were comparatively well off. We moved back to Detroit when I was ten. I'd been in a little town where I was the smartest in the class and my father was on the school board, so I was resented. I got in the habit of trying to be inconspicuous. When I was sent to a huge school in Detroit, I waited for them to find out I was good, but they never bothered. It took a long time before I learned to come out of that shell.

"I went to Wellesley. I liked the music department, and the place was physically beautiful. I studied counterpoint and orchestration and composition, but there was no ear training, and my ear deteriorated from lack of use. I spent a lot of time in Boston listening to jazz and singing with groups like the Crimson Stompers, at Harvard. I had started singing in high school and had had some coaching. Summers, I sang a little at an outdoor dance place near a cottage we had in Belle River, Ontario. Father had to ask the leader if I could sing with the band. Billie Holiday was my idol, and I saw Mildred Bailey in Boston. After graduation, I supported myself as a secretary in Boston, at thirty-five dollars a week, and I collected cover charges at the tables for George Wein at his Storyville Club. I sang with Lester Lanin-type groups. Then I went to New York, and through a friend of my parents I found a steady job in a clip joint in Union City. There were four chorus girls, too, and all of us were expected to sit with the customers, but I was bad at that. I was bad at everything. I had no stage presence. I was scared to death. I didn't know what to do with my hands. So I retreated to Boston, and worked in lounges where it was safe and dark. I slowly got tough. I worked with a piano player in Boston who couldn't read, couldn't keep a beat, couldn't transpose, couldn't play the songs of the day, and hated to play the piano. And that gave me a great musical independence—I learned to sing with anyone, anywhere, under any conditions. I made my first record in 1954, and moved to New York for good. Things began to happen. I made a record for Riverside in the spring of 1955. It got great reviews, and John Wilson listed it as one of the albums of the year, along with Marlene Dietrich and Bing Crosby and the *Oklahoma!* soundtrack. I won a *Down Beat* poll as the best new singer in 1956, and I worked at the Village Vanguard. But I didn't believe any of it. I considered myself a college kid who happened to sing. I didn't accept myself as a grownup. I had gotten married and my husband managed me, but we split up and I was convinced I couldn't go on working without him. So I started at the Lane Theatre Workshop, on West Forty-sixth Street. It was run by a brilliant man named Burt Lane, who, by choice, is now driving a cab. Jean Shepherd sent me there. I began to learn about people: that they didn't always mean what they said, that you didn't have to tell the truth—or, rather, that other people didn't. I learned something about alternatives in life and art. I began to come out of my dream world. I had a twenty-dollar flat in SoHo, which I had to heat myself. I made a movie full of liberal dialogue about Castro called *Rebellion in Cuba*, and I had a substantial part in *Finnegans Wake*. The first was shot in Coral Gables and I was the leading lady and it was terrible, and the second was made in New York and shown maybe twice. I got a job with the Stanley Woolf Players in the Catskills. Tony Curtis came out of them. We stayed in Liberty and went out to a different hotel every night. It was thirty a week and room and board. I did some Off Broadway and a lot of summer stock, and I generally worked enough to get unemployment. During this time, I sang when I got the chance—at a family place called Vinnie's Horseshoe Bar, in Astoria, and on a concert tour with Marian McPartland and Mose Allison. I sang all the time in elevators and supermarkets and on the street. But I didn't work anywhere as a singer after 1964. I had become a housewife and an actress in California, and after that I got my master's in drama at San Fernando Valley State College, and came back East and taught speech at the American Academy of Dramatic Arts and acting at Hofstra College.

"In 1972, I ran into a piano player I'd worked with fifteen years before. He said he was in a little place at Fifteenth Street and Irving Place, and I sat in with him for three hours one night. I began dropping in there, and I started going back to Vinnie's Horseshoe one or two nights a week. Things have multiplied, and it looks as if I'm back singing again. I did Alec Wilder's radio show and had two engagements at Michael's Pub. But I will always keep my hand in the theatre.

"There is nothing as sensual as singing. Acting is quite different. There is the teamwork, and exploring another person and his emotions and responses. In a way, everything is given to you—costumes, script. The words are not your responsibility but the character's. Singing is nothing but *me*, and years ago I was swamped by the responsibility of it. Now my face isn't locked, my back isn't frozen. I can let my face and my body go with what I'm singing about. Phrasing has to do with the meaning of the lyrics and the play of rhythm against rhythm. Even when I'm singing a phrase, I hear two or three other ways of singing it. I like to think the unheard ways are subliminally present. Singing is a very physical act. It's your lips and teeth and mouth. It's your chest, where the sounds are resounding. The meaning and textures of the words you sing roll around in the body before they gather and go into the microphone. It all comes back through your ear, and that's another sensation, as is moving any part of your body while you're singing. I didn't realize how marvellous the textures of the consonants are until I studied speech with Arthur Lessac. He likens the letters of the alphabet to the instruments of the orchestra. 'B's, 'P's, 'D's, 'T's, 'K's, and 'G's are drumbeats. 'Ch's and 'Dg's are cymbals. 'L's are saxophones. 'R's are trombones. When you say a word like 'asks,' you fall in love with English and realize what an extraordinary language it is. Something happens at a good performance. The singer and the audience hold it together. When Teddi King was at the Carlyle, singer and song and audience became one. I'm totally involved when I'm singing, but part of me is always monitoring the rest of me to keep the content and the precision in balance. I want to weave as nearly complete a tapestry as I can. Singing isn't playing an instrument. There are words, and words have their own music. They also have meaning, which should be expressed in your tone, your timbre. The tone you employ is consciously not always the most beautiful. When you sing 'That man of mine ain't comin' home,' in Irving Berlin's 'Supper Time,' you should use a sound that expresses anger and sadness and finality. Some singers sing every song with the same tone, and that is like speaking in a monotone. If you're going to do 'Down in the Depths on the Ninetieth Floor,' you should have some rage and bitterness in your tone. You should not have a beautiful sound. There are many singers who *use* music. I resent that. Music is sacred. The song has to control the performance. Doing anything else—employing this or that trick—to make the audience applaud is an outrage. Then you are making them applaud *you*.

"A good accompanist must know that he and the singer are there to serve the song. He should love songs, and I mean music *and* words. And he should be free of attitudes and prejudices and prejudgments—like if it isn't a so-called jazz tune, it isn't good. The most important quality musically in an accompanist is rhythm, and that means being able to swing and to control the motion of the song. A good accompanist has to know how to go along with your phrasing—whether to play counterpoint or echo you or put in a little resonant harmony. Just one right note from a good accompanist can send you flying. An accompanist like Jimmy Rowles *listens*, and with one like Dave McKenna I can almost *see* the power descending from Heaven and coming out in those hands."

Let It
Be Classy

Alberta Hunter

The singer Alberta Hunter was waiting in a studio to rehearse
with her accompanist, Jimmy Rowles. A contemporary of
Bessie Smith and Ethel Waters, and an immediate descendant
of Ma Rainey and Sophie Tucker, she was about to resume a
career she forsook for practical nursing after her mother's
death in the mid-fifties. She had the time to sing again because she had recently been retired by the Goldwater Me-
morial Hospital, on Roosevelt Island, where she had worked
for twenty years. But her return was largely accidental, and
she explained it this way: "A while ago, Bobby Short had a
party at his house for Mabel Mercer, before she went to
sing in England, and he invited me—Lord, I've known Mabel
nearly fifty years. Mr. Charles Bourgeois was there, and
I saw him sizing me up, and pretty soon he asked me to sing
something, which I did, real soft. He told me, 'You should
be out working again, with that voice and all your experience,' and right away the next morning Mr. Barney Josephson of The Cookery called and asked was I interested

in singing for him, and I was so nervous I dropped the phone. I never appeared at the Café Societys, but I always knew his reputation. I went down there a few days later and sang, and he said, 'I want you to go to work for me right away.' "

Head-on, Alberta Hunter is egg-shaped, and sideways she is Egyptian. Her face is lean and tight and handsome, and her gray-black hair is swept back into finger-size braids. Her brown eyes are clear, and she talks in a staccato, near-stuttering fashion, often tapping a listener's hand for emphasis with a sharp, woodpecker finger. She was wearing a fitted dark-khaki dress with military pockets, and she declared that she loves to dress casually. Chris Albertson, the author of a biography of Bessie Smith, arrived, and was followed by Rowles. Rowles came up to Alberta Hunter, and she smiled and asked him how he was. Sleepy and emery-voiced, he said, "Fine, baby doll."

"I was just saying how I hate to dress up, how I love to be casual. When I was entertaining, I spent a lot of money on clothes, but after my mother passed I gave them away, all those pretty gowns and slippers. I could die, because they're back in fashion. But how was I to know I'd start singing again and need them? I'll just get myself a smart cocktail dress, and I'll be all right."

Rowles riffled through a pile of sheet music, and Alberta Hunter said, "I'm going to sing songs in six languages—Italian, French, Danish, Yiddish, and German. And English. I've got the music here for the Yiddish song and the French song, but I want to start today with a blues—my 'Down-hearted Blues.' I want to make it a *real* slow blues so there's plenty of time to get the story out."

"I used to work for an arranger on the Coast named Marty Paich," Rowles said, "and he'd always tell me he wanted me to play real 'fonky.' "

Alberta Hunter picked up her music and put it on the piano. She stood in the crook, next to a microphone. Rowles applied some Tacky-Finger, a non-slipping ointment, and Alberta Hunter folded her hands in front of her, raised her head, and scanned the room as if she were about to address a packed house. "Ladies and gentlemen," she said in an even contralto, "I'm going to sing a song I wrote in 1922, when most of you children weren't born. I recorded it on the Paramount label, and Bessie Smith used it for her very first Columbia recording, which sold a million copies. It's called 'Downhearted Blues.' "

Jimmy Rowles played a four-bar introduction, and Alberta Hunter began the famous lyrics: "Got the world in a jug, stopper right here in my hand. Got the world in a jug, stopper right here in my hand. The next man I get, he's got to come under my command." Her voice was steady and rich, and her vibrato betrayed none of the quaveriness that often besets older singers. Her phrasing was legato, and once in a while she used a high, almost falsetto cluster of notes which recalled Ethel Waters. There is a burnished, accreted assurance and depth and color in Alberta Hunter's singing. At first, she stood nearly motionless. She moved one knee on the beat, and occasionally she raised her right arm and smoothed the air with her hand. Then she went into a fast "When You're Smiling." She began rocking from side to side, and slapped one thigh on the afterbeat. She bounced up and down, her slightly bowed legs moving like springs, her long arms walking at her sides. A slow "He's Funny That Way" was next, and was followed by another blues, "Handy Man" which starts, "That man of mine has a scheme. That man of mine has a scheme. It's amazing the way he handles my machine." Rowles was brilliant. He paralleled her melodic lines, echoed them, cushioned them. He gave her rhythmic nudges when her time faltered, and he played rich and dense chords behind her. But he used this complexity sparingly, and it set off the purity and simpleness of her voice—a jungle framing a smooth clearing. Rowles suggested a break after a swinging "My Blue Heaven," and they sat down. He asked Alberta Hunter when she first came to New York.

"Why, it was in 1923," she answered, hooking a cardigan sweater around her shoulders. "I had got to thinking that I should look for higher ground, that I'd gone as far as I could in Chicago. So I left there on a Saturday, and by the following Wednesday I'd replaced Bessie Smith in New York in a show called *How Come?* I'd never been on a stage, but I was young and I just walked out there and had no fear. After, I wasn't sure whether or not I had cut a hog —messed up—but I knew I was all right when that audience yelled and stomped and Sophie Tucker and all them who were out there gave me a standing ovation. I was in *How Come?* about a year, and then went into a show called *Change Your Luck*, at the George M. Cohan. I went back to Chicago for a while and worked at the Royal Garden and the Phoenix and the Sunset Café with Earl Hines. I also worked in Cincinnati, at Michaelson's, and I met a waiter there named Willard Saxbe Townsend. He was handsome. He had beautiful eyes. He'd been in the Army, and I don't think he owned anything but that uniform. I married Willard and we went back to Chicago. I had a little apartment and my mother was staying with me. I was too embarrassed to sleep with my husband with my mother there, so I slept with my mother. Willard wanted to be a waiter where I was working, but I didn't want any part of that, so I took a vacation and went to Monte Carlo, where I found a job in the Knickerbocker Café. I never got back with Willard, and eventually it made a man of him. He got a degree, and when he died he was head of the redcaps' union in Chicago and the only Negro on the executive board of the C.I.O. I've never given getting married again a thought. I stayed abroad four years, and there wasn't any place I didn't go. Noble Sissle helped me get into England, and I lived in London in the same house as Marian Anderson, at 17 Regent's Park Road. She was there getting her middle register straightened out with Miss Amanda Aldridge. Marian was always a mama's girl, but she was completely unspoiled— and talk about a lady! We always got along, and she used to say God made me and threw the pattern away. But she didn't have any soul then, and we used to say things purposely to hurt her so that she'd feel things and get some

soul, and she did. I auditioned for the English company of
Show Boat, and got the part over a white woman named
Maisie Ayling. I played Queenie. Edith Day was the star
and Sir Cedric Hardwicke was Cap'n Andy and Paul Robeson was Joe. My old friend Mabel Mercer was in the
chorus. Paul was unassuming, like people used to be to each
other in the South. When he sang 'Ol' Man River,' his voice
was like a bell in the distance, and people would scream.
The night King George and Queen Mary came to see us,
Paul got off pitch, and he never got himself back on, and
afterward he cried like a child. I stayed with *Show Boat*
eleven months, and then I went to the Grande Carte in
Paris. I learned French at Berlitz and got a part in a show
called *Vive Paris!* There was a scene with a huge birdcage
filled with women dressed like birds, and I sang 'Les
Oiseaux.' Then I went on the road—to the Natural Scholar
in Copenhagen, the Excelsior in Alexandria, the Continental
in Cairo, and the Femina in Athens. I worked Les Jardins
des Petits Champs in Istanbul and the place in Vienna where
Hitler used to drink beer. I came back to England in 1935,
and I used to sing 'Time on My Hands' for the Prince of
Wales at the Dorchester. I also did some broadcasts from
London to New York, and when I came home I was on
WEAF and WJZ and on the 'Lower Basin Street' show,
before Dinah Shore took over. I was in a lot of vaudeville
in the thirties, with people like Seymour and Jeanette, and
Ada Brown, who was like a chubby baby. I worked at the
Hot Feet Club down here, and in 1939 I took part in *Mam-
ba's Daughters* at the Empire, at Fortieth and Broadway. It
was Ethel Waters' show, and since she's gone and can't
speak for herself I shouldn't say a word, but she sure gave
me a hard time. I guess I outsang her, because she put everything but the kitchen stove on me. But I forgave her a long
time ago, and a year before she died she sent me a message:
'Tell old Flossie'—which is what she called me—'hello and
take care of herself.' I joined the U.S.O. in 1944, and was
with them off and on until the day my mother died. I took
the first Negro unit overseas during the war, and when

Marshal Zhukov gave General Eisenhower a medal Eisenhower sent for me to come and sing. I worked the E.T.O. and the South Pacific and the C.B.I. and Korea. The last club I was in in New York was the Bon Soir, when I was studying nursing."

Alberta Hunter stood up and smoothed her dress. "Come on, Jimmy. It's time to work again." Rowles applied more Tacky-Finger and sat at the piano, and they went into a rousing "Sunny Side of the Street." Alberta Hunter's springs went up and down, her arms walked, and every eight bars or so she snapped her head. Another Hunter blues, "Working Man," followed "My man is old and very thin. But there is plenty of good tunes left in an old violin." A slow "Pennies from Heaven" came next, then an even slower "A Hundred Years from Today," and she finished the rehearsal with a rocking "A Good Man Is Hard To Find." Rowles jumped up and shook her hand and laughed.

"We got to pick some of those tempos up, Jimmy," she said. "They drag."

"You pick 'em up, I'll be right there."

"An old lady shouldn't drag her tempos," she said.

"Old lady!" Rowles shouted. "You know what you are, Alberta? You're a *sprinter!*"

She laughed and slapped him on the chest, and Rowles put on his jacket and told her he'd call her in a day or two. Chris Albertson joined her, and she looked at him. "Do you know when I started singing? I started singing when I was about twelve years old. But I had to be born first, and that was in Memphis, around 1895. I had two sisters. One was older and called La Tosca, and one was younger and a half sister, and her name was Josephine Beatty. I used her name when I recorded in 1924 with Louis Armstrong for Gennett, because I was still under contract to Paramount—Josephine Beatty, accompanied by the Red Onion Jazz Babies. My mother was born in Knoxville. She was tall and slender and very strict, but she did everything she could for her girls. She used to carry me around on a pillow when I was little, because I was so sickly. She was a very tidy person, and she scrubbed the paint off when she cleaned. 'Get away from me, you're filthy dirty,' she's say to me when I came in off the street. Which is where I got my nickname—Pig. My mother worked as a chambermaid for Miss Myrtle and Miss Emma in a sporting house on Gayoso Street. My father, Charles Hunter, was a Pullman porter, but he died before I ever knew him. We girls stayed most of the time with my grandmother Nancy Peterson, who also looked after all my cousins. She was a dainty little lady, who wore a shirt-waist with a velvet front. Her rent was five dollars a month, and when they threatened to raise it a quarter she said she would move, and they backed down. She used to tell me over and over, 'Keep busy, be a lady, keep your clothes clean even if they're raggedy, stay away from whiskey, and never put a cigarette in your mouth. And do your work the best you can.'

"I went to Chicago when I was eleven, thereabouts. My mother had sent me to the store with a dime and a nickel to buy bread. I ran into my teacher, Miss Florida Cummings, and she said she was going to Chicago, had a pass for the train, and would I like to go, just like that. Well, I used to sing in little school concerts, and my music teacher had told me I could sing. I had heard you could make ten dollars a week in Chicago singing, and I had been building that up in me. So I thought I better go to Chicago and get some of that ten. I told her wait and I'll ask my mother. I ran and hid a little and came back and said yes. I knew my mother would think I was over at my friend Irma's house when she missed me, because I stayed there a lot. In Chicago, I knew enough to find the daughter of a friend of my mother's named Helen Winston. She was so surprised when she saw me. 'Sit down, Pig,' she said. 'What in the world are you doing here? You hungry? Miss Florida should have known better than to bring you up here like this'—and on and on like that. When she quieted down, she took me out to Hyde Park, where she worked, and got me a job as second cook for six dollars a week, room and board. She took the braids out of my hair and put me in dresses to make me look older. Right away, I sent my mother two dollars so she'd know where I was. I hadn't been there very long when I started sneaking out to a place called Dago Frank's, at Archer and State. It was a sporting bar, and when I tried to sing they told me to get out. But they finally gave me a chance, and I worked there a year and ten months. The hours were eight to twelve, for five dollars a week. I learned songs from the piano player like 'Melancholy,' which became known as 'Melancholy Baby,' and I also sang 'All Night Long' and 'Where the River Shannon Flows.' The next place I sang was Hugh Hoskins'. The dangerous element, like Give-a-Damn Jones, hung out there, but so did the pickpocket women, and they did everything in their power to show me how to live a clean life. Tack Annie was considered the cleverest pickpocket anywhere. She was a master. She had some sort of hook concealed in a front tooth, and by leaning over near a gentleman she could pull a diamond stickpin right out of his tie. But she was an ugly girl. Fact, she looked like a mule with a summer hat on. When I wrote 'Reap What You Sow,' I was thinking of some of those rough types.

"Hugh Hoskins' was a small place, which was enlarged because so many people came to hear me sing the blues. Then I was offered twelve dollars a week at the Panama Café, at Thirty-sixth and State. It was owned by Izzy Levine and Mr. Shaw. It was a long place, and there was an upstairs and a downstairs. There were five girls upstairs with a piano player and five girls downstairs with a piano player. Nettie Compton, Bricktop, Florence Mills, Cora Green, and Mattie Hite were downstairs, and Glover Compton, who was marvellous, was their piano player. Each one did her own thing, and the downstairs was swank, dicty. Upstairs, we had Nellie Carr, Goldie Crosby, Twinkle Davis, Mamie Carter, and me, and George Hall was the piano player. Nellie Carr did the splits, and Mamie Carter had a cute little dance. Twinkle Davis had legs like Marlene Dietrich, and Goldie Crosby had her jazzy little way. And

I sang the blues. The people would pass on by Bricktop and them to come up and hear us. I worked next door at the De Luxe Café, too. Freddie Keppard played trumpet there. He was something—a big fellow. He had an old derby, and he put it over the bell of that trumpet and he'd make the hair stand up on your head. He could play loud and he could play so soft you couldn't barely hear him. Then I went across the street to the Dreamland Café, which was owned by Bill Bottoms, who later became Joe Louis's dietitian. He paid me seventeen dollars and fifty cents a week. Joe Oliver had just come up from New Orleans—this was around the First World War—and he had Sidney Bechet and Lil Hardin and Minor Hall. Oliver was big and dark, and I don't think he had any sight in his left eye. Leastwise, he sometimes wore a patch over it. But he was a lovely fellow. Later, after he brought Louis Armstrong up from New Orleans, I recall them playing 'Jerusalem' in harmony with their mutes and without any rhythm section—just the two of them floating along—and it was unbelievable. I think a little chill grew up between them when Louis began to be recognized. The Dreamland was a big square place, and the musicians played on a balcony. I'd sing down on the dance floor, and when I'd finish a song I'd throw up my hands so the musicians would know. All I'd have to do was hum a new song for them to get it. The dance floor was large, and the center was made of glass and had a light under it. There was no segregation, and every sort of person came in—the pickpockets and society Negroes and politicians and gamblers. The gamblers were kings, and they were allowed to raise a fog, which is letting people go as far as they like. Al Jolson came to hear me do 'St. Louis Blues' and 'Mammy's Little Coal Black Rose.' Sophie Tucker came to hear me do 'Someday Sweetheart' and 'A Good Man Is Hard To Find.' Later, she'd send her maid Belle for me to come to her dressing room and teach her the songs, but I never would go, so her piano player would come over and listen and get everything down. But I was crazy about her as a singer, and she influenced me. I was at the Dreamland about five years, and while I was there I started recording for Paramount, through Mr. Ink Williams. Fletcher Henderson accompanied me, and so did Eubie Blake and Armstrong and the Original Memphis Five, with Phil Napoleon and Miff Mole. I remember the thick brown wax discs they recorded on and the wax shavings falling on the floor as I sang. The Memphis Five was white, and they could *go!* I was the first black singer to record with a white band. I recorded my 'Downhearted Blues' about a year before Bessie. I never so much as said good morning to her, but I heard her sing. That voice carried from here to downtown. She was crude, raucous, and her clothes were a little clowny, a little extravagant. She just stood there, and when she started 'Nobody Knows You When You're Down and Out' you could feel her big heart going. When Bessie opened her mouth, it was the end of a perfect day. Of course, Florence Mills became just as big a star as Bessie, but she was the opposite. She was a hummingbird, and dainty and lovely. Her little voice was as sweet as Bessie's was rough, and it was like a cello."

Alberta Hunter buttoned her sweater and looked around. Her expression was serene and bemused. "I better think about getting along, go home and finish the song I'm working on. It's a blues, which means to me what milk does to a baby. Blues is what the spirit is to a minister. We sing the blues because our hearts have been hurt, our souls have been disturbed. But when you sing the blues, let it be classy. Singing a ballad, the meaning of the words runs in my mind all the time. In 'Sunny Side of the Street,' I *see* that sunshine and I'm really as rich as Rockefeller. I'm always trying to tell a story, and I want my words to be understood. I've been writing blues and songs all my life. A new song will often come to me at three or four in the morning. I'll hold it in my head and later that day dash downtown and get somebody to set it down on paper, because I don't know a note of music. Eddy Arnold sang my 'I Want To Thank You, Lord.' Dinah Washington did 'What's the Matter, Baby?' and Ella Fitzgerald did 'Downhearted Blues' and so did Mildred Bailey, who made a crackerjack record of it. My new song is called 'I Want a Two-Fisted, Double-Jointed Rough-and-Ready Man.' " She sang, "I want a man who won't let his children play with neither dog nor cat but will bring in a skunk or a lion and say, 'Here, kids, play with that.' I just got the melody to it this morning."

Majesty

Joe Turner

Joe Turner looked more like a wayfarer resting by the road than a performer in a night club. The master Kansas City blues singer was seated on a low stool next to the grand piano in Barney Josephson's Cookery. He held a microphone in his right hand, but he rarely used it. He waved it in small circles above his knee, he marked time with it, and sometimes at the end of a stanza he brought it to his mouth and delivered a shaking basso tone. He had a cane in his left hand, and he leaned on it and occasionally tapped the floor. His clothes were a motley of Kansas City and Los Angeles, where he lives: a dark-blue suit with high-waisted pants and a broad belt, an orange sports shirt with a black design, and huge new sensible shoes. Turner was sitting down because he had gained a lot of weight during the preceding decade and wasn't able to stand for long. "It was all that travellin', all that eatin' heavy food on the road for thirty years, that put this weight on me," he has said. "I guess my legs won't take it because of an accident I had in Kansas

City when I was twelve years old. There was a fire, and I had to jump out of a second-story window of the apartment we lived in, and I broke everything. Doctor said I'd never walk again. I was in the hospital two months, and after that I crawled around on the floor a year until I got sick of it and grabbed onto chair backs and pulled myself up and started learning to walk again. But some weakness must have been left, and that's what's botherin' me now." The rest of Turner, who is over six feet tall, is unchanged. His black hair is combed flat, and his face is still a boy's face—a collection of round shapes arranged around large laughing eyes. His voice is the same, too, except that it has deepened. It is a huge voice, a pre-microphone voice—a Bessie Smith voice that was trained a long time ago to carry across fields and down streets and through ballrooms. Turner has been called a blues "shouter," but shouting implies effort and even strain. All Turner has to do when he sings is open his mouth and get out of the way.

Turner is probably the greatest of blues singers, stretching from Blind Lemon Jefferson and Big Bill Broonzy through the marvellous Jimmy Rushing and down to the white English rock singers. Not all his compeers have understood the blues. Some have treated them as dirges. Some have chanted them. Some have sung them as if from a pulpit. Some have intoned them the way Carl Sandburg did his poetry. Some have laughed at them. But Turner has invariably sensed that this simple twelve-bar (not always), three-chord (not always), tonic-subdominant-dominant (not always) form is capable of assuming all sizes and shapes. He sings of every human condition—loneliness, comedy, death, irony, fear, joy, desperation—and he does so in a godlike manner. He hands down his lyrics with his great voice. Sometimes they are intelligible and the passions harbored in his words stare through, and sometimes he pushes his words together, lopping off the consonants and flattening the vowels so that whole lines go past as pure melody, as pure horn playing. Before Turner, most blues singers recited their words. The melodic content of their blues remained unchanged from

stanza to stanza. They used the same notes, the same inflections, the same rhythms. But Turner improvises, for he was
raised among the great musicians who lived in or passed
through Kansas City in the twenties and thirties: Lester
Young, Ben Webster, Pete Johnson, Count Basie, Buster
Smith, Jo Jones, Clyde Hart, Walter Page, Mary Lou Williams, Dick Wilson, Ben Thigpen, Hot Lips Page, Jack
Washington. He speeds up his time and slows it down. He
hustles his words along and spaces them out. He roars, then
drops to a soft rumble. On a fast blues, he quickly and repeatedly raises and lowers his voice a tone or a tone and a
half, and a line like "You so beautiful, but you got to die
someday" jiggles and jumps past so quickly that we almost
miss *what* he is saying—the story of humankind in nine
words. On a slow blues, he bends his notes into domes and
parabolas, lets them glisten briefly before he cuts them off,
pauses, and starts the next line. There is no waste in Turner's
singing. He rarely indulges in the luxury of a vibrato, and if
he does it is short and flat. He is a percussive singer, and his
lines fall like blows. The colors in his voice match his brevity
and rhythmic force. It is a slate-gray voice that pales at
faster tempos and grows almost black when he slows down
for a line like "It's three o'clock in the morning, and the
moon is shining bright." His voice has heft and agility and
streamlining. Turner's imperturbability and cool give his
singing a don't-give-a-damn air, but that seeming insouciance
is the secret of his majesty.

So Turner sat and sang, an extraordinary presence, whose
only motions were small and sporadic. As the numbers went
by—some of them anthems like "Roll 'Em Pete" and "In the
Evening When the Sun Goes Down," and "Cherry Red"
and "Every Day" and "Wee Baby Blues"—he nodded almost imperceptibly, from lower right to upper left, or kept
time with his cane, or marked the afterbeat with the microphone. There was no hint of his discomfort ("Sittin' on that
stool half the night makes you want to almost cry") or of
his nervousness at not having sung much in New York since
1942, when he last worked for Barney Josephson, at Café

Society Downtown. He kept his eyes lowered; he looked at the audience between numbers quickly, but after he had counted off the time for his pianist, Lloyd Glenn, and his guitarist, Wayne Wright, he dropped his eyes again. At the end of the set, he heaved himself to his full height, bobbed his head at the audience several times, and made his way toward his table at the far side of the room—a house being moved down a road.

Most days, Turner and Glenn, who were sharing a room at the Gramercy Park Hotel, loaded themselves into a cab and went to The Cookery for lunch. One afternoon, when the lunch people had cleared out, Turner pushed the table away to make himself comfortable, and Glenn, who had eaten with him, moved to another table and studied some sheet music. Glenn is slight and smiling, and the white hair at his temples flashes. He is a remarkable blues pianist—a special breed that is all but gone. His accompanying stays out of Turner's way, but his melodic lines and chords frame and embellish Turner's sharply different moods. Through a judicious use of blue notes and tremolos and a strong and original left hand, he rocks. If he is asked a question, he talks fast, and is happy to say that he was born in San Antonio in 1909 and learned to play boogie-woogie and blues piano from such local masters as John and Pudson Harris (who were brothers), Little Archie and Big Archie (who were unrelated), Bubber Howard, and Will Woolrich. Turner doesn't recall having worked with Glenn, but Glenn is positive they recorded together in Los Angeles in the fifties in an upstairs studio for a label that had a picture of Liberty on it. Barney Josephson put away some silver he had dried and sat down and said, "Joe, I remember walking into Café Society one night and there were Albert Ammons and Meade Lux Lewis and Pete Johnson and you—four giants—lined up at the bar. I must have looked glum, because you said, 'What's the matter, Pops, you down?' You reached in a pocket and took out a bean and said, 'Now, in my hand is a bean and in that bean is a face as alive as you and me, and you can talk to it and tell it your troubles.' You made a fist and then opened it and slapped your hand down on the bar so that the bean landed under it. 'Everybody cover my hand with your hand,' you said, and we did—Ammons and Johnson and Lewis and me, a pile of black and white hands. Then you started mumbling something like 'Bajabajeboojiborumbayahoojie,' and you stopped and said, 'All right! Take away your hands. You got nothing to worry about now. Everything's just fine.' Well, I laughed like hell and suddenly I realized I felt wonderful."

Turner looked at Josephson and smiled and let loose a descending "Yehyehyehyeh, man" that sounded as if he were singing. Indeed, there is little difference between his speech and his singing: one walks and the other lopes. "Walter Winchell gave me a flash on his radio program about that bean and what it could do for people," Turner said. "I got the bean from an African who worked in a place where he walked on broken glass and swallowed fire and didn't hurt himself. He told me to rub it and say that mumbo-jumbo and the bean would do anything, as long as I believed in it. After Winchell gave me the flash, people started asking me to rub the bean and help them do this and cure that, and I went wild, it was causing me so much trouble. Finally, it scared me to death to have so much power, and I put the bean in the toilet and pulled the chain. But I believed anything in those days. I thought New York was out of sight. John Hammond had heard Pete Johnson and me at the Sunset Club in Kansas City and sent for us to come to New York and play at that Carnegie Hall concert. I believe it was 1938. We met Albert Ammons and Meade Lux and we all got to be great friends. John Hammond gave us money every week, and we stayed up on Seventh Avenue at the Woodside Hotel. He told us to have a good time, and that he'd get us a job, but he didn't. So we went back to Kansas City, and waited for John Hammond's call. Everybody laughed when we got home—'Hey, you couldn't make it in New York City, man.' We'd say, 'Yeh, yeh. We just waitin' for John Hammond to call us back,' and they'd shake their heads and laugh again. Then John Hammond called, and we went to work at the Café Society for four or five years, and I didn't get back to Kansas City until 1950."

Turner ordered a sugarless black-cherry soda and swung one leg up on the bench he was sitting on. "I was born in Kansas City on May 18, 1911, and I was the baby of the family. My sister Katherine Turner—now she's Katie Bryant, which is her married name—is three or four years older, and she used to say my mother spoiled me. My mother made her take me wherever she went. But I like to bug her all the time because I was devilish. My father was a cook at the Baltimore Hotel and the Muehlebach Hotel, and he was a fisherman, too. He caught crayfish in the lakes and ponds and streams, and they had claws almost as big as a lobster's. But I don't know too much about him. He was killed by a train when I was three or four, and I was raised by my mamma and my grandmother. Raised, I guess—'cause I run pretty much from the time my daddy was killed. My mother was a tall woman, and a very beautiful lady. She was real light. She died five years ago in the house I bought for her in L.A. She was from La Belle, Missouri, and my father was from San Antonio. I never did ask where they met. After my father died, my mother worked in a laundry, pressing shirts. Until I went to school, which was the Lincoln, about ten blocks away, I stayed with my grandmother, who lived across the street. She was tall, too—a reddish-looking woman, like an Indian. She was my mother's mother, and I knew her as Mrs. Harrington. She had ten daughters. I never heard my mother sing a note, and she didn't play no music, and my father didn't, either. But ever since I was a kid I had singing on my mind. I started singing around the house. We had records—Bessie Smith and Mamie Smith and Ethel Waters. Ethel Waters is the only singer I ever adored, and I met her after I got to be a man. I used to listen to an uncle by marriage named Charlie Fisher. He played piano in a night club, and he also played on a piano in the hall downstairs in our house, which was like an apartment building. He taught me the new tunes, and I listened to two other uncles, who played guitar and banjo and violin. I was about thirteen by then and had gotten over my accident. We'd duck school a lot—I didn't get past the sixth grade anyway—and go down to the river and fish and swim. Or I'd go down from the house a block or two in the morning and find one of the blind blues singers standing on a corner. I'd stay with him all day and we'd cover the town. He stopped on corners and sang and I passed a tin cup. We went into restaurants, too, and when I was old enough I sang along. I made up words—blues words—to go along with his guitar music, and later, when I was singing with a band, I could sing for two or three hours straight and never repeat a lyric. Those blind blues singers would make quite a bit of change during the day, and they'd pay me fifty cents. I did that off and on for two or three years, but I can't remember those singers' names. My mother didn't worry none about me when she found out—only did I have a hat on under that hot sun. I did all kinds of jobs. I shined shoes and sold papers and worked with a man had a double team and a wagon and hauled paper boxes and like that. I'd lead horses around the stockyard and make a couple of bucks, and I had me a job in a hotel cooking breakfast for the waiters. I learned how to cook from my mother and grandmother—least from watching them. I'd cook bacon and eggs, and fried potatoes, and grits, which we called mush. They kept it on ice until it got real hard and then I'd slice it and cook it like potato pancakes. I sang a lot on the streets, me and a bunch of the boys. They played gas pipes with one end covered and an old banjo and big crock water jugs. They blew across the mouth of those jugs and made that bass sound to keep the beat—boom, boom, boom! When I was sixteen or seventeen, I started hanging around the Back-biters' Club, which was on Independence Avenue. I sat outside and listened to Pete Johnson play the piano. The windows were painted over on the inside, and during the day I sneaked in and scraped off enough paint so me and my buddies could watch the people dancing at night. My brother-in-law was the doorman, and his job was to shake down the customers, search them to see if they were carryin' guns—anything like that. I couldn't get in at night with him around, but when he took another job I drew a mustache on my face with my mother's eyebrow pencil and dressed up in my daddy's hat and one of his shirts. I was already tall, and I'd slip the hat down over my eyes and go in with a crowd. The musicians would tell me, 'Go home, little boy,' but I'd bug them and say I could sing, and finally one night they let me. There was no mike in those days, but I got up there and sang blues songs, and they were surprised I could keep time so good and that I had such a strong voice. I sang a couple of songs and the man who owned the joint liked them and the people liked them. The man asked me how old I was, and I told him twenty, and he looked at me and said, 'Your mama know where you are?' and I told him my sister did, and I started working there on weekends. He paid me two or three dollars."

Turner yawned and examined a watch on his right wrist, which had Los Angeles time, and at a watch on his other wrist, which had New York time. "I got to walk me around some before my legs die," he said, and worked himself to his feet. He rocked down to the front of the room, his shoulders sloping like eaves, turned, and rocked back. When he reached his bench, he looked at it for a while and swung himself down with a swift unbroken spiral motion. "Oh me, oh my," he said, then shouted, "Glenn! Hey, Glenn!" as if he were on one side of Grand Central Station and Glenn on the other. Glenn looked up and smiled and came over. Turner peeled a twenty off a wad of bills and handed it to him. "Get me some change for that, please, Glenn. You said you got to go to the drugstore, so find me three big Vicks nose drops. They got that other stuff, the other jive, don't let them talk you into it. But don't come back with nothin', without some kind of nose breather. My throat dries up with all this singing and carryin' on."

Turner rested his hands on his cane. "The Backbiters' Club had an upstairs and a downstairs," he said. "The bar was upstairs and the music downstairs. I sang with Pete Johnson, and he had Murl Johnson on drums and a saxophone player. We moved to the Black and Tan club, which had been a furniture store and had a balcony and all. An Italian named Frankie owned the place, and he wanted to make me the manager. I said I didn't want that but I would get the entertainers and the waiters if he'd let me learn to tend bar. The bartender was Kingfish, and he was older. Part of my job was to get the bootleg whiskey and part was to take off my apron and sing with the band when things were quiet. Kansas City was wide open, and sometimes the last show would be at five in the morning. After Prohibition ended, we moved to the Cherry Blossom, at Twelfth and Vine. It had been a theatre, and it had a great big dance floor. George E. Lee had a band there, and his sister Julia Lee played the piano and sang. She was a beautiful brown-skinned woman with personality plus. The floor show had a comedian named Rabbit and a shake dancer, which was like a dancer in burlesque. Me and Kingfish still tended bar, and we had a ball serving beer in those big heavy glasses. We were at the Cherry Blossom two or three years, and then I left town with Pete Johnson's band and travelled to Chicago and St. Louis and Omaha and back to K.C. again. We moved around, back and forth and in and out, but we never went too far from home. My mother was running an apartment building at Eighth and Charlotte then, and I'd show apartments for her, but I always kept one back for me and my gang. I went into the Sunset Club. Piney Brown ran it, and I was a bartender and still sang. When the place was empty, the band would play real loud and I'd go outside and sing through one of those big paper horns, up and down the street, and the people would come. I thought I was somebody when I got enough money together to buy a paper horn and a baton so that I could direct the band when I wasn't singing."

Glenn gave Turner his nose drops, and Turner checked his New York watch. "Hey, Glenn. I believe there's still time for you to take your nap." Turner's voice sank, and he went on talking, almost to himself. "You get out there and flag a cab and get in and when you pay the man he got to have his tip, too, and then you get in another cab and come back here to go to work and you pay again and tip him, and it's startin' to cost a lot of money." His voice trailed off. He peered around the room and his gaze stopped at the piano. "The reason I look down at the floor so much when I'm singing is if I look at the people I forget what I'm doing, which bugs the devil out of me. But I can see the people out of the top of my eye and see how they take what I'm doing. If they don't look happy, I change things around and sing something different. When I push the words together, it's because the piano player might be playing too fast and I don't want to get left behind. I'm in trouble if they go on without me. It's like the merry-go-round. I don't want to fall off the horse and have to wait until it comes around again." Turner was silent. He was running down. He looked at Glenn, who had got up and put on his coat. Turner stood up and headed for the front door of The Cookery. "I settled in L.A. in the fifties, but I been on the road pretty much ever since. Paul Williams, Dusty Fletcher, bands like that. I worked with Helen Humes, and we got to be big rock-and-roll stars. It wasn't but a different name for the same music I been singing all my life. By the fifties, Pete Johnson, who was my buddy, went his way and I went mine. He finally settled in upstate New York before he died. I been married three times. I had a little boy, but heart trouble took him. Whatever money I've made the wives about got it all. I'm married again, to Patricia Sims. We been married five or six years, and I still work around L.A., and Norman Granz has had me to make some records for him, so I keep busy. It's my life. Singing's all I know how to do."

Just a Singer

Helen Humes

The first great gathering of American singers happened, without much warning, between the late thirties and the early forties. Suddenly there they all were—on Fifty-second Street and at the Blue Angel and the Village Vanguard and the Café Societys and the Paramount, as well as on records and the radio and in the movies. It was bewildering and almost impossible to plumb and compare and categorize them all; there were too many, and an astonishing number were good. But two pecking orders, each with its own devices and accoutrements, immediately fell into place. In the first were such megaliths as Bing Crosby and Frank Sinatra and Dinah Shore and Doris Day, and in the second such masters as Mabel Mercer and Billie Holiday and Mildred Bailey and Johnny Mercer. Of the second, one of the most durable was and is Helen Humes, who bears comparison with Mildred Bailey and Billie Holiday. But Bailey and Holiday and most of their compeers are dead or retired or poking around in the ruins of their voices, while Helen Humes is singing as well as ever. That is a sufficient kindness, but she is also sharing with us a style of singing and of performing that is almost gone. She came out of the pre-World War One South, mostly self-taught and with the sounds in her head of horn players like Dicky Wells and Jonah Jones and of singers like Bessie Smith, whom she heard twice at the Lincoln Theatre in Louisville. It was a kind of singing that we can barely imagine learning now. It preceded the microphone and by necessity demanded a strong voice, Ciceronian diction, and an outsize presence. The singer was *alone* onstage. It was also a kind of singing that relied on embellishment and improvisation, on an adroit use of dynamics, and on rhythmic inventiveness. The singer jazzed his songs. Only a handful of such singers are left, and none is better than Humes.

Helen Humes had fifteen minutes before going onstage at the midtown night club where she was working. She was wearing a sleeveless black gown whose halter top was emblazoned with sequins and a lot of gold brocade. She is a pretty woman. Her features are regular and arranged just so, and her lifted chin italicizes them. She wears her hair in a short, dark cloud, which is lighted from beneath by her classic smile. Her hands and feet are small, though the rest of her is mapped out in expansive meadows, sharp drops, and roomy valleys. But extra pounds are to singers what nimble feet are to boxers; they add depth and range to the attack. Unlike many Southerners, Helen Humes has a loquacity that is frequently tempered by thought. "This is the first long gig I've had in New York since I worked for Barney Josephson more than thirty years ago, at Café Society Downtown," she said. "It was 1942, and I had just left Count Basie. I was tired and my health was getting bad. I was nervous with all that bus travel, so I went home to Louisville to sit around and rest. Then I went to work at Café Society, where I stayed into 1943. Then I went up to Fifty-second Street, I think at the Three Deuces, and then I was down at the Village Vanguard with Eddie Heywood.

While I was there, Derby time came around and I wanted to be South, so I got Pearl Bailey to take my place for a few weeks. Well, I haven't returned to New York for any time until now, and Pearl went on from the Vanguard to the Blue Angel to Lord knows where, and she hasn't looked back since. Me, I went out to California with Connie Berry, who was a piano player. I did five seasons with Jazz at the Philharmonic. I worked in Hawaii in 1951, and in 1956 I went to Australia with Red Norvo. I went back to Australia in 1962 and again in 1964, when I stayed ten months and they tried to make me a citizen. I travelled to Europe my first time in 1962 with a raft of blues singers like Brownie McGhee and Sonny Terry and T-Bone Walker and Memphis Slim, and in 1967 I was at Shelly's Mannehole and Red Foxx's club, in Los Angeles. But Mama got sick and I went home. When she died, not long after, I decided to quit singing, and I took a job in a munitions factory in Louisville. I was there two years and I made gunpowder. You had to stand on wet concrete floors and there wasn't a lot of heat in the winter, but I was having the best time. Being an only child, which I am, you like crowds, you like people. Then, in 1973, Stanley Dance came to Louisville and invited me to the Newport Jazz Festival, but I told him I didn't know if I could sing anymore. I was scared to death to even try. But I came up and I stayed close to Nellie Lutcher the whole time, and she pulled me through so good that five days after I sang at the Festival I was on my way to France to work for four weeks. A year ago, I went back to France and sang at Newport again and did a week here at the Half Note.

"Talking about my mother, I was blessed in both my parents. My mother was a schoolteacher named Emma Johnson. Her father and mother had come from Lancaster, Kentucky. He was a full Cherokee and a medicine man, and she was half Cherokee, half Irish. My father was from Knoxville, Tennessee, but I didn't know much more than that about him. He just died, at the age of ninety-six, so I think his parents, who I never met, must have been slaves. I was in New York doing some business when he passed. He was in the hospital in Louisville, and he'd had a seizure of the flu but was recovering real nice. I went over to Jimmy Ryan's the night before I was to leave, but I felt strange. Roy Eldridge hollered to me from the bandstand, 'Hey, Humes, come up here and sing.' But I told him I just didn't have it in me, and I went back to where I was stopping to go to bed, and found out the hospital had called and my daddy had died just when I was at Ryan's. My father was known as Judge, or J. H., for John Henry. He was one of the first black lawyers in Louisville, and he was always doing something for other people. 'You have to have friends. You can't live in this world by yourself,' he'd always tell me. My mother never worked again after I came along. We had so many good times together—popping popcorn and making ice cream and playing games. When she died and I made up my mind to quit singing, I sold my piano and my record-player and my records so I wouldn't be reminded or tempted, and that was it. Or I thought it was."

Helen Humes laughed and pushed herself to her feet. She went over to the piano. Her accompanists—Ellis Larkins and Benny Moten—were already warming up. She said something to Larkins, who immediately leaned back and released one of the mystical sprays of hand signals that he prefers to words. He played several left-hand chords, and Helen Humes turned around, detached the microphone from its cradle, smiled, and, standing by the piano as easily as if she were in her living room, began "There Is No Greater Love." During the first chorus, her voice and the song kept missing one another. Her vibrato ran a little wide, she cracked a couple of notes, and her dynamics were uneven. But everything settled into place in her second chorus, and she fashioned an impressive series of embellishments. She started phrases behind the beat and then caught up. She used melismatics. And she worked her way back and forth quickly and cleverly between near-shouts and langourous crooning. She has a light voice strikingly reminiscent of Ethel Waters, but she insists that no singer influenced her.

Humes' voice has a dark, fervent underside, which appears when she sings the blues and which Waters lacked. Her phrasing is hornlike. She takes daring liberties with the melody, particularly in her second choruses, and she keeps close guard on her vibrato. Like all pre-microphone singers, she can shout at will, and she can also slipper along just above a whisper. She is a master of rhythm. When it pleases her, she drags behind the beat, passes it and falls back on it, and unerringly finds those infinitesimal cracks that exist between beats. But there is nothing deliberate or contrived in her style. It is elegant primitivism, and it has a sunny, declarative quality. Her next number was a medium-tempo, shouting version of "Please Don't Talk About Me When I'm Gone," and then she did an attentive "Every Now and Then," a song she delights in and renders much as it was written. A hymnlike "Summertime" was followed by a cheerful "Birth of the Blues," complete with its verse, and a rocking—and for her—quite moody "Gee Baby, Ain't I Good to You." She kept accumulating and then sweeping away little piles of notes all through "I Can't Give You Anything But Love," and she finished her set with a dramatic reading of "If I Could Be with You One Hour Tonight."

She sat down and wrapped a sweater about her and mopped her face. She cleared her throat and banged her chest with her hand several times. "I think I still have some of that cold I toted up here from Louisville," she said. "But I feel better singing now than I ever did before. My voice used to be so clear when I was younger, and people tell me it's gotten real clear again. I'm happiest when I'm singing—particularly if I have a good accompanist like Ellis. I just sing the way I feel. Most of my songs come out differently each time, but there are some I try and do the same way each time. I've been called a blues singer and a jazz singer and a ballad singer—well, I'm all three, which means I'm just a singer. And I've always been myself. I didn't model myself on anyone when I started out. Somebody'd tell me to listen to So-and-So's record, but I'd only listen, if I listened at all, *after* I had learned the tune myself.

"I got started as a singer almost by accident. After I had graduated from high school, I took a two-year business course and got a job as a secretary in the First Standard Bank, which was the first black bank in Louisville. During my vacation, I went to stay with Margaret and Luke Stewart, in Buffalo. They were Louisville friends, and Luke was one of the greatest guitarists I ever heard. I went up there for two weeks, but I didn't get home for two years, because I took my first work in Buffalo as a professional singer. I'd been singing and playing the piano most of my life. I fiddled with the piano as soon as I was tall enough to reach the keyboard, and after I had tried the clarinet and the trumpet, which I didn't care for, I took piano lessons from a very good German teacher, who had me going in the classics. I sang in church from the time I was little, and I sang and played piano in the Sunday school Bessie Allen ran at the Booker T. Washington Center. You could learn any instrument there, and that's where Dicky Wells and Jonah Jones and Bill Beason started. When I was fourteen, Sylvester Weaver heard me sing. He was a blues singer who had recorded on the Okeh label. He told Mr. Rockwell at Okeh about me, and Mama took me to St. Louis and I recorded 'Black Cat Moan' and 'A Worried Woman's Blues.' I believe J. C. Johnson was on the piano. A while later, I made some more records in New York, including 'If Papa Has Outside Lovin'' and 'Do What You Did Last Night,' both of which I'd like to hear now so I could sing them again. But I never kept any of my records, because I never thought they was as good as they could have been. That was all the recording I did then, except the Okeh people asked me would I like to go on tour. But Mama said no.

"I worked at the Spider Web, in Buffalo, and then over at the Vendome Hotel, where I was with Al Sears' band. He's retired now and doesn't do *nothin'* but play golf. I must have been in Buffalo a year, and then I went on to Schenectady, where I did my first radio program, with two white girls, and on to Albany and Troy. I went home after that, and a few months later I rejoined Al Sears at the Cotton Club in Cincinnati. This was in 1937. One night, Count Basie stopped in and offered me a job. He said he'd pay me thirty-five dollars a week, but I was already making that without having to travel, and Basie wasn't much yet anyway, so I said no. Well, Al Sears *did* go on the road, and we ended up at the Renaissance Ballroom, in Harlem, where John Hammond heard me, and this time I *did* join Basie. Billie Holiday had just left him, and I went with the band at the Famous Door, on Fifty-second Street, in 1938. That was when Basie really exploded, and when he had Buck Clayton and Dicky Wells and Lester Young and Jo Jones. I didn't have any trouble being the only woman in the band. I did my singing and went home and read a book and went to sleep. When we went on the road down South, the chances were good we wouldn't be allowed to eat in any decent place, so I started doing the cooking. I had my pots and my hot plate with me, and I cooked backstage. When I'd left the band and was at the Café Society, the phone would ring and it would be somebody from the band passing through, and he'd say, 'Hey, Humes, this is So-and-So. What you got cookin', honey?' Jimmy Rushing was my best friend in the band. He was full of fun and had stories in his head twenty, thirty years old. We'd sit on the bandstand together and he'd tell me things and we'd start laughing, and Basie would get mad. Later, when I was in L.A., Jimmy'd call when he was in town and I'd cook and we'd spend the day eating and drinking and playing cards and laughing."

Ellis Larkins and Benny Moten were in the middle of an intermission set, and Helen Humes paused to listen for several minutes. "This is the first time I ever worked with Ellis—the first time I ever *met* Ellis—and he is something else," she said. "People told me before, 'Look out for Ellis, he's difficult.' But he's all right. Since I don't have anybody in my family left to look after, I might as well spend the rest of my time singing. But I'll keep Mama and Papa's house in Louisville. Thank heavens a neighbor recently moved into it to keep an eye on it! Down there in the summer, the little boys in the neighborhood make a path through my yard going after the peaches on my three peach trees. They come early in the morning and call up, 'Miss Helen, my mama wants to make me a cobbler, so can I pick some peaches?' One little boy came back and back and finally a tattletale told me, 'Miss Helen, he selling those peaches.' I've had a very happy life, and I wouldn't do it otherwise. I even got married once and survived. I married a Navy man in 1952, but I haven't seen him since 1960. He wanted to settle in Japan, and I told him, 'Fine, and I'll be right here if you ever come back.' I don't even know where he is now. I haven't made all the money some people think I have, but anytime my friends are in distress and if there's anything I can do for them, I do it. I guess I'm like my father that way, and I guess he was like *his* father that way. At least, that's what Mama always told him."

It's Detestable
When You Live It

Ray Charles

In Los Angeles, midway between Beverly Hills and Watts, there is a small, factorylike two-story building that is occupied on the ground floor by the Urban League and on the second floor by R.P.M. International. (The initials stand for Recordings, Publishing, and Management.) The building, of gravy-colored stucco, blends easily into a nondescript, old-fashioned residential area dotted with small stores and small businesses. It has windows only on the ground floor, it is rectangular and flat-topped, and, except for its partly glassed-in front, it is as expressionless as a brick. But its insides, like a poker player's thoughts, are startling. A flight of stairs carpeted in Florida orange climbs from the foyer to an orange-and-white reception room containing a switchboard, a desk, an orange-haired receptionist, a leather sofa, a couple of leather chairs, and a coffee table displaying the newest issues of *Down Beat*, *Billboard*, *Hollywood Reporter*, and *Record World*. Two facing doors open into yellow halls. At one end of one of the halls, off which are a

dozen brightly colored cubbyhole offices, is a spacious yel-
low-and-blue-and-black recording studio, equipped with a
piano and an organ, clusters of microphones, and a control
room, jammed with glistening sound equipment and resem-
bling the cockpit of a jet plane. At the opposite end of the
hall are adjoining mogul offices. In the bigger one, three of
the walls are painted yellow and the fourth is made of rough
brown cork blocks. The wall-to-wall carpet is bronze. A
dreadnought V-shaped table-desk, set before a high-backed
leather chair, faces the door, and arranged around the walls
are an upright piano, a television set, a long leather sofa, and
a card table ringed by chairs. An enormous moonlike lighting fixture is set into the ceiling. The smaller office is a fre-
netic twin: the desk and the cork wall and the sofa are black
and the floor has brilliant red carpeting. This one is occupied by Joe Adams, the executive vice-president of Ray
Charles Enterprises, which is the heart and mind of R.P.M.
International, and the bigger office is occupied by Adams'
friend and boss, Ray Charles, the unique blind singer, pianist, composer-arranger, music publisher, recording executive, and promoter.

Charles *is* the American Dream. He is wealthy and world-
famous and inordinately gifted. But none of this, his talents
excepted, was given him. He was born in sub-log-cabin pov-
erty in the Deep South at the start of the Depression, he
went blind when he was seven, he was an orphan at fifteen,
he has been harried by drugs, and he is black. Despite all
this, he has solved the Midas-touch-versus-artistic-integrity
problem with extraordinary grace. He is, in his naked, powerful manner, in a class with Billie Holiday and Bessie
Smith and Louis Armstrong, and, in a country that has
never counted jazz as one of its blessings, he is admired by
every class, color, and creed. There is no one explanation
for this miracle. Perhaps it is because Charles almost *touches*
his listeners' emotions with his voice, perhaps his wild, to-
the-bone singing offers a safety valve, a purgative in a tur-
bulent time, perhaps the iron honesty of his voice helps off-
set our haywire morals, or perhaps it is simply because he is

a zealously concentrated performer whose singing and presence and timing form a flawless hypnotic force.

Charles' style, fed by a bottomless emotional well, has many sides. He can sing anything short of lieder and opera. He has recorded standard popular songs, country-and-Western music, down-home blues, American anthems such as "Old Man River" and "America," novelty numbers, rock and roll, the Beatles, and folk music. He works with equal ease in front of a small jazz band, a big band, vocal groups, choruses, and strings. (The sound of his pinewoods voice tearing along over violins and a choir is one of the wonders of music.) He can shape his baritone voice into dark, shouting blocks of sound, reduce it to a goose-pimpling whisper, sing a pure falsetto, yodel, resemble Nat Cole at his creamiest, and growl and rasp. He is always surprising. Yodels follow deep-throated rasps, he dwindles from stark recitative to a soft, fleeing moan, he rocks along way behind the beat and then jumps into metronomic time, he yells asides to his accompanists or the audience between words, he bends and cracks and splits notes in treasonous places, and he is a master of melismatics. Insofar as it is humanly possible, he never repeats himself; every performance of "Georgia on My Mind" is minutely and marvellously different. He is his own best accompanist, playing a piano that ranges from the country blues to a clean, Nat Cole single-note style, and he is a competent, swinging alto saxophonist. His compositions, gospel-flavored and often funny, are a natural extension of his singing, and so are his arrangements, with their economy and their affecting voicings.

His appearance is deceptive. From a distance, he looks frail and spidery. He has a shuffling, bent-kneed walk, and at the piano he sways wildly from side to side or rears back to the point of falling over. A steady smile and big, ever-present dark glasses mask his face and make him seem smaller than he is. But close up he is tough and compact. He has wide, boxers' shoulders and a flat, trim waist, a high forehead, close-cropped hair, flaring cheekbones, and a jutting, stony chin. His speaking voice is deep and guttural and hand-hewn. He talks quickly and his language moves between sunny, sprawling Southern colloquialisms and lofty Northern abstractions. He is startling on the telephone; he literally barks and grunts. And he is in constant motion—reading from a Braille notebook with one hand and holding a telephone with the other, lifting his head and shooting out his chin, wringing his hands or clapping them softly together, and standing up for no reason to do a little hopping dance and then abruptly sitting down.

In recent years, Ray Charles the singer has become the cork bobbing on top of the Ray Charles Show, which appears, on a concert basis, in night clubs and concert halls around the country and in Europe. This generally opens with his big band, a seventeen-piece group that is the equal in precision and fervor of any current big band. The band plays a batch of instrumentals, and the Raelets, a comely female vocal quartet, sing several numbers. After an intermission, and with the audience kneaded and ready to rise, Charles himself appears, and sings and talks and plays his way through a dozen or more numbers.

In January, February, and March, the Ray Charles Show rests. But Charles spends most of this time in his office at R.P.M., arranging bookings for the coming year, managing his small stable of young talents, memorizing lyrics, walking down the hall to record, consulting with Joe Adams, holding staff meetings, editing tapes, considering new songs to record, talking on the telephone, and granting interviews.

"Most days, I get here late, but I stay late, till nine or ten," he says. "I can get more done between 5 and 10 p.m. than I can during the day. Actually, one of these days I might run for senator or governor and get a bill passed to make the working day from about 11 a.m. to 7 p.m. The way it is now, most people don't go to bed until twelve or one anyway, and the next day they walk into that office at eight-thirty or nine evil. My way, you'd read your papers and drink your coffee and leave your house nice and new about nine or ten. You couldn't pay me to live in New York, which is just the nerve center, the money center. I like the slow pace out here, which is more like the pace of Europe.

"I've never been able to understand why the people where you live should be any problem. Anyway, what the hell difference does it make if you're colored or white? I just want to be treated fair. And I don't want to be treated better because I'm blind. When I went to school, there just weren't any books about us. It was George Washington and it was just like a dictatorship. We were told what we could learn and that was it. Hitler couldn't have killed all the Jews he did by himself. He had to condition other people. It's the same with black people. That nappy hair. You've been taught it's bad. You're conditioned. Same thing, why is it *black*mail instead of *white*mail? I've seen a commercial on television where they have these two cars testing gasoline, and the white one always goes the furthest. When you have people who have been *made* to feel imperfect, the problem is how to teach them they *are* good, that it has nothing to do with color. After all, a lot of the whites who first came over here were outcasts, religious or from prisons, but people just want to control other people. Now the Northern people always say, 'Did you see what they're doing to the Negroes in Alabama or Mississippi? ' but they're doing the same thing up here, only they're sneaky about it. Down South, at least they're open. They *tell* you. I wonder what would happen if Christ *was* black. 'His face shall shine like patent leather and His hair be like the wool of a sheep,' it says somewhere in the Gospels. I would like to see what would happen if He came back and He came in the wrong color. I'm not one who worries about coming back. I don't quite believe God is going to take the good people and raise them from the dead, but if He did I don't picture Him needing to take the nothings of the world and raising them, too. The bad people would just be the dust the good people walked over.

"When I'm on the road, I'm home in pieces—two or three days here, a week there. It's not so bad. It used to be a lot worse. I'm fortunate enough to have my own plane. I can do four hundred miles to a gig in an hour instead of spending the whole day in a bus. We have a Viscount turboprop —a four-engine prop jet with Rolls-Royce engines. The way we have the configuration of it, I have a lounge and sleeping area in the back, and in the rest of the plane we took out a lot of the seats and spaced the remaining ones plenty far apart. There are roughly thirty-five of us on the road, but the plane could hold sixty-four. Before that we had a Martin 404, a two-engine job, which could carry about forty. And we have a little twin-engine Cessna 310, which holds about five people. I like to fool with radio and engineering when we're flying, but I believe I could set down a plane if I had to without killing myself. I might tear a wing off, but I don't believe I'd kill myself. Anyway, we have two full-time pilots, and we've been lucky. Once, we were in the Cessna—there was the pilot and co-pilot and a couple of friends—and we were coming into the Oklahoma City airport. It was freezing outside and the heater that is supposed to defrost the windshield broke and the windshield was coated with ice and we literally couldn't see a damn thing, even when we got down to two hundred feet. So we circled and circled, and of course the more we did the more ice the plane picked up and the heavier she got, and on top of that we were running out of fuel. Then suddenly a hole appeared through the ice on the windshield. It looked exactly like somebody had taken an icepick and made it. It was a miracle. So the pilot could see the strobe lights and he brought us in. The pilot I had then, Tom McGarity, like to broke his neck on the ice on the ground when he got out of the plane, but he didn't panic up there. We've never had any trouble with the Martin and the Viscount. Lightning hit the Martin once and went straight through the plane. It made a *bang* and scared the hell out of everybody, and you could see it come out the other side."

There was a knock on the door, and Joe Adams came in. He is over six feet tall and slim and Broadway-handsome. He has arching eyebrows and a small mustache. His hair is combed flat. He is a clotheshorse, and he was wearing a green V-neck sweater, a turtleneck shirt, and olive pants. His voice is low and even, and he speaks with B.B.C. precision.

"I have the band list," he said to Charles. "Contract time is coming up. You want to put your thoughts on who you want and who you don't?"

"Go ahead," Charles said.

Adams sat down on the edge of the desk, swung one leg slowly back and forth, then began to read the roster. (Some of the names have been changed.) "Leroy Cooper."

Charles nodded.

"Wallace Davenport."

"He's all right," Charles said.

"George Jay."

"I'd like to do a little research on that."

"Henry Thomas."

"Yeh. I'd love to have him back. He's a preacher, that one."

"Jim Abbe."

"I could go either way."

"Richard Gachot and Barklie Henry."

"I *have* to have them."

"John Masterman."

"I'm going to do a little research on that, too."

"David Griffin."

"I believe we can live without him."

Adams read the rest of the list, Charles made his yeas and nays and maybes, and Adams left.

"Out of seventeen guys in a band, it always works that you have just six or seven who are the key men—the men who concentrate and work with the younger cats and keep the outfit straight and sharp. It's very hard for a guy in the band to skate on me. I can hear every horn, every note. Musicians are not the easiest people to handle. A lot of times I make people nervous in the band, so I try and be a little close with them. If there is something personal a musician has on his mind and he can't handle it, he can come to me, and fine. I've always wanted a big band to work behind me. I like the sound. You can make a small band from a big band, but you can't make a big band out of a small band. I'm a person who takes his time, and when I could afford a big band I put one together. And I've been fortunate enough to maintain everything new I've tried. It was my mother who taught me that patience.

"Her name was Areatha and my father's name was Bailey Robinson. My name is really Ray Charles Robinson. Sugar Ray Robinson was a powerful man when I was coming up, so I took my first and middle names and dropped the last. Then, of course, later I ran into the other Ray Charles, the choir director, but it hasn't been any trouble, outside of getting each other's mail once in a while. I was born in Albany, Georgia, in 1930. September 23rd. But my parents moved to Florida when I was two or three months. We moved about forty miles east of Tallahassee to a little bitty place called Greenville. My father worked for the railroad, cutting and repairing the crossties and connecting the steel. But he was also a mechanic and a builder. He could build anything. In the South in those days, you learned to do many things to make a living. We were poor people in every sense of the word. My father taught me if you ever get your hands on a dollar you always keep enough to get home on and you never let that dollar become your word. If your word is no good, your money isn't, either. He could go downtown and give his word anywhere, and that was it. If he said he'd be somewhere on Monday at eight in the morning, it was Monday at eight, not Tuesday at ten or eleven. I try and do that. I work maybe three hundred jobs a year, and in the last fifteen years I've missed just three jobs and I've only been late six times. My father was what they used to call a 'good nigger.' But he was no Uncle Tom. He just wanted to be left alone, and he was not interested in chasing some white woman. He was very well respected. If a white man liked you, he liked you and he'd do anything in the world for you, and that was the way my father was treated.* My mother was a sweet lady. She cooked and worked for white families, and she made all our clothes. And she had a strong feeling about independence. Just because I was blind, she'd tell me, didn't mean I was stupid. 'One of these days I'm gonna die and you're gonna have to take care of yourself,' she'd say. So I was taught to wash and scrub and cook and rake the yard and make my own bed. I'd cut wood, too, which caused a situation in the church, where they got to saying that my mother was making that poor blind boy cut wood when a piece of wood might fly up and hit him in the face, so she went and told them that even when a man with sight cut wood sometimes a chip flew up and hit him in the face and even if he saw it he couldn't move fast enough, and that quieted them. If I hadn't of been taught by my mother, I wouldn't be anywhere. I was brought up not to beg. Even now, I wouldn't beg nobody for *nothing*. If we had a little extra, we knew it, and if we didn't, we knew it, and nobody said a word. I think my mother killed herself working with my father to make ends meet, and I'm sorry she didn't live long enough to see me become something.

"I was born with good sight and I didn't start having trouble with my eyes until I was five. It started by my eyes running like hell all the time. Not tears—it was too thick. It was more like mucus, and when I'd wake up in the morn-

---

* In *Brother Ray: Ray Charles' Own Story*, by Ray Charles and David Ritz, published by Dial in 1978, Charles says this of his father: ". . . To tell the truth, I wouldn't bet a lot of money he and my mother ever were married. . . . The old man wasn't part of my life. He was a tall dude—I remember that. But he was hardly ever around. . . . Sometimes he came to see Mama, but not very often. He was so big and she was so small that people often confused them for father and daughter."

Ritz feels that the Charles in his book is authentic and that the Charles in this chapter is, by Charles' design, for white folks. But the version and voice here ring right, whereas Ritz's overtell, tape-recorded Charles does not.

ing it was so thick I'd have to pry my eyes open. The pressure began to build up behind my eyes and there was a pain like the pain you get in your head when you stay up for two or three days and don't sleep. Then my horizon began to shorten up. The local doctor was not a specialist, but he did the best he could. He gave me drops and told me to stay out of strong light. But it got worse and worse, and when I was seven I was stone-blind. I often think of my parents having to watch all that. It was probably glaucoma. At least, that's what doctors I've talked to since say it sounds like. Glaucoma used to damn near kill people, but now thirty per cent get their sight back and forty get partial sight. I remember many things about seeing: the way the sun looks, the moon looks, my mother looks, and the colors, the standard colors, the mother colors—red, green, black, white. I remember the sunsets. I only use my memory of seeing if an occasion calls for it. If I want to buy some clothes, I can get a true picture of the colors using my memory of the mother colors. Normally, I don't look to the past for instruction. There are so many things you can see without the eye, and ninety-five per cent of seeing is unimportant anyway. I know what this desk is like and what this chair is like and what a woman is like. I don't have any trouble with food or taste, and I've never been a heavy eater anyway. I like a good cup of tea and about a gallon of milk a day. And there are things I don't want to see, like people lying in the street with their heads bashed open. I see as much through touch as most people do through seeing. The majority of the time there is someone with me, but I'm not sure that wouldn't be the same if I could see. The first time I came to New York, I came alone, and before I had money I did everything by myself. Now, I don't drive a car, but I don't ever care about driving a car. I ride bicycles and motor scooters. I've been known to do that. I'd love to ride a bicycle in Central Park when I'm in New York next time—go out with two or three people and they'd ride right near me and talk. We used to ride bikes in the hills around home, but I don't recommend it for everybody.

Your senses don't become better by theirselves. You develop them. I used to shut myself up in a hallway and take a golf ball and throw it against the end of the hall and try and catch it before it passed me coming back. I'd judge where it was by the way the sounds bounced off the walls, the same way when I was walking down the street by myself, my step would make an echo and the echo would get louder and louder when I approached something big, like a building. *Every*thing makes a sound, even crêpe-rubber soles on a rug, but you have to train yourself to pay attention all the time. If I came to a very busy intersection, where the traffic sounds got mixed, I'd get myself in among a bunch of women, and when they crossed I'd cross with them. And I caught the trains and buses and planes by myself. If you hand the ticket man a one-dollar bill for a five-dollar ticket, he'll let you know, and I'd always ask for my change to be counted out in singles. I don't think in all the years I was out there by myself that anybody beat me for a penny.

"We were tough kids then, stuck in that little town in the woods in the South, where they gave you castor oil for everything. It was different from now and it helped you later in life. If we fell out of a tree and knocked our wind out, we got up and kept running. If we got cut, we'd stick some clay dirt in the cut, or a cobweb, and that would clot it. If we had boils, we'd take the thin skin from just inside the shell of an egg and put it on the boil, and it would burst, or we'd take a hot brick from on top of the stove and pee on it and create steam and the steam would burst the boil. We'd make tea out of honey and lemon and sassafras, and it would sweat out a cold, and if we ate too much candy we'd take castor oil and a few drops of turpentine, and, baby, it worked. And we ate a lot of hard foods—raw sweet potato and hard pears and coconuts and the meat from sugarcane. They'd exercise your gums."

Charles leaned back in his chair and lifted his glasses slightly, rubbed his eyes, and pushed the glasses back in place. He seemed to be staring at the light in the ceiling.

"I love to work with young people. I wished it was that

one day a week, Sunday or something, the big newspapers would devote space to what the young people do *right*. Let the young people *know* that they don't have to rob a bank to get in the news. If I was in charge of a newspaper, I'd find out what the young people are doing that's *good*, and print it, so they'd know we care about them. It's like my feeling about drugs. What I did is done and that's that. I've been talking about drugs to the papers and everybody for a long time, and I could continue to talk about it for thirty more years. But if you make a mistake and rectify it, you don't want to hear about it the rest of your life. I'm no missionary or pope and I'm not trying to reform anybody. I did it and it's done and over and that's that."

Charles picked up the telephone and asked when the Sony people were coming to demonstrate a portable motion-picture camera. He put the phone down, missed the cradle by an inch, and jiggled the receiver into place.

"Well, I didn't start school until I was seven, when my parents sent me to the St. Augustine School for Deaf and Blind Children, in St. Augustine. It was a state school. Before that, my mother, who was not the most educated woman in the world, taught me. She taught me the ABCs and a little arithmetic, and she taught me how to print. I can still print today. I can't write, but I can print. I was treated very fair in school. I was normal there, happy there. In September, the state bought your train ticket to get you there, and in June they bought you another one to get you home, but at Christmas your parents had to buy the tickets. The school went through the tenth grade, which is what I was in when my mother died. I was fifteen. She had some sort of gastric disorder. She'd eaten a sweet-potato pie or sweet-potato bread and she blew up like a balloon overnight and she died the next day. I came right home. I couldn't cry right then, and I couldn't eat for three weeks, and I almost died for it. My father was never the same after that, and he died—they said from diabetes—not long after.* My

* See note on page 58.

mother was thirty-three and my father about forty. There were just no medical facilities outside of the local doctor. The nearest hospital was forty miles away, in Georgia. If you got sick you went to bed and Mrs. Reynolds or Miss Jones or Miss Williams, ladies in the area, they took turns and stayed up with you at night.

"My mother had brainwashed me to the point where I had to be independent. There was no point in living off this aunt or that uncle, and anyway they was mostly living in places like Baltimore, which was a *long* way away. But I knew some people in Jacksonville through my mother— Lena Mae and Freddy Thompson. I agreed to live with them because I could pay them something. I'd go out and play piano at tea parties and such and make five dollars and give half to them. They fed me and took care of me. I had picked up my first piano at home. There was a little café next to us and it was run by a man named Wylie Pitman. He had a piano there and he was of the boogie-woogie school—Meade Lux Lewis and Albert Ammons and the like. When he played, I'd run in and listen. He must of taken note. He would let me sit on the piano bench next to him and bang on the keys. I didn't know *nothing*. He would tell me, 'Play it, play it. You're doing fine.' I'll always love that man for that. He just let me bang on the piano, and one time when I was about six and I was losing my sight and there were some other people in the café, he called over to me and said, 'R.C.'—which is what people called me—'I want you to play like you played yesterday.' I had the nerve to get shy when I couldn't play a damn thing anyway, but I sat there moving my left hand back and forth and banging with my right and they clapped just to make me feel good. From that point on, I loved to play music. By the time I was seven I could play little tunes, one finger, then two fingers, and I had always loved to sing from the time I was tiny. Mr. Pitman had a jukebox and I'd hear those blues by Big Joe Turner and Tampa Red and Big Boy Cruddup and Sonny Boy Williams. When I got to school, I started studying. I was an excellent musical student. I studied Chopin and

Mozart and Bach. Beethoven had a lot of feeling, but Bach was nervous, with all those lines running against each other. Classical music is a great foundation for playing jazz. You play correctly, with the right fingering. With classical music, you play exactly what the man wrote, but in jazz, when you get rid of the melody, you put yourself in. So every time I thought my teacher wasn't listening, I played jazz. And I listened to Goodman and Basie and Ellington and Erskine Hawkins and Andy Kirk and Lunceford and Tiny Bradshaw and Artie Shaw. Shaw got me interested in the clarinet, so I took it up, along with the alto saxophone and a little trumpet. Shaw had more feeling than Benny Goodman, and I loved his sound. And of course my favorite pianist, then and now, my idol, was Art Tatum.

"I stayed with the Thompsons about six or seven months. I had worked a little in Jacksonville in Henry Washington's big band, but he didn't need me, so I went to Orlando and got a job with Joe Anderson, who had a sixteen-piece band. I wrote arrangements for him and I sang. I've done a lot of arranging and occasionally I still do one. I can hear the whole arrangement in my head, note for note, and I just sit down and dictate it. We didn't work too often, and there were times when I was sustaining myself on beans and water and crackers, and it came to be a heavy proposition—a malnutrition thing. I can really understand how people can get chained into situations like that, how people can get stuck in a web and can't get out. Men sit and stare and women become prostitutes. I was one of the fortunate ones. I had this little profession and I did get out of it. But it was total hell twenty years ago, with the race thing and being blind, too. It's easy for people who eat warm food and sleep in warm beds to talk about it, but it's detestable when you live it. I stayed with Anderson three or four months, then I went to Tampa. I knew a guy worked in a music store, and one night he took me to this little club and I sat in on piano with a hillbilly group, the Florida Playboys. Their piano player was sick and I got the job. It was a strange thing. They were white, but they were always nice to me.

Every night, they took me home, and when the girls came up and talked to the fellows I didn't feel left out. I wasn't interested in chasing no white girl. My only interest was music and getting my hands on some money. I always loved hillbilly music. I never missed the *Grand Ole Opry*. It was honest music, not cleaned up, and it still is. They don't sing, 'I sat there and dreamed of you'; they say, 'I missed you and I went out and got drunk.' I learned how to yodel by being around the Florida Playboys. Then I went with a small combo led by Manzie Harris, and after I had saved my money with him for seven or eight months I decided I wanted to get out on my own, go to a nice-sized city the furthest from where I was. I was afraid of New York and Chicago. I had a friend, and we took a map of the country and he traced a straight line diagonally as far as it would go and it hit Seattle. I didn't know anybody there and nobody had sent for me, but I got on the bus. I got to Seattle at five in the morning. I went to a little hotel near the bus station and I was so tired I slept twenty-one hours. When I woke up, I asked downstairs what time it was and the lady said two o'clock. I thought it was two in the afternoon. She straightened me out and I asked where could I go to hear some music and she told me about a place, a private club, called the Rocking Chair. I took a cab and knocked on the door and told the man I'd heard they was having a talent night. I pleaded with him and he said, 'O.K., you look older than eighteen. Come on in.' When I got my chance, I sang 'Driftin' Blues,' and they went wild. People from various clubs in town were there and the man from the Elks Club heard me and two days later I had a job there. I put together a trio—the McSon Trio, with Gosady McGee on guitar and Milt Farred on bass. I'd known McGee in Florida, so that was one of those strange coincidences. I never thought of calling the group the Ray Charles Trio, and when we got our first money—three hundred dollars—I divided it evenly, even though I was the leader. I didn't know anything. We worked at the Elks three weeks and then the Rocking Chair man approached me and asked me to come and work for him, and instead of giving two weeks' notice, which I didn't know about, either, I told the Elks man the whole story and he said, 'All right, you have told me the straight of the thing and I am very happy for you and you go.' I spent most of my time in Seattle in the Rocking Chair, but I also worked the Black and Tan, the 908, and the Washington Social Club. And I got married, but it didn't quite work out. We had a little trouble with the girl's mother. She thought I'd never amount to anything, and rightly, I guess. I don't blame her. But once we were married and every time there was some disagreement between us this girl she'd call her mother and her mother would lay it on me on the telephone. I didn't have any poise and I wasn't as nice as I am now. So I said some wrong things. But I think it could have worked out if the mother had said, 'Settle your own fights; it's between you-all now.' "

The Sony people were announced, and Adams ushered in a blond girl, a white man, and two black men. Charles stood up, swayed from side to side, and moved into the middle of the room, his right hand extended. Adams introduced the girl, Miss Becker, and the white man, Mr. Rice. The black men, Terry Wilcox and Howard Moorehead, are friends of Charles. Charles shook hands all around.

"I first met R.C. in a little country town in 1955," Wilcox said to Miss Becker.

"I remember," Charles said.

Rice was unpacking a big camera, a portable tape recorder, and several other pieces of equipment, and he was down on his knees.

"Come on over, Ray," said Moorehead.

Charles squatted. Rice said, "This is the battery charger and it has instructions."

"I don't like instructions," Charles said. "I like to find out myself how things work."

"This is the plus post and this is the negative," Rice said, and guided Charles' hands. He moved them quickly and lightly over the area, and Rice explained how everything worked. Charles nodded and began loading the tape machine himself. "Stay still, sweetie," he said to a reel of tape. "If I can get you on, we'll have some action."

Then Rice showed Charles the camera. His hands scuttled over it like big hermit crabs.

"The lighting is kind of poor in here," Moorehead said.

"I like it that way," Charles said. "Generally, I don't have any lights on at all. This is the one place in the building where we save on the electric. O.K., people. I appreciate all this. You get everything fixed up and I'm gonna take some pictures."

The Sony people shook hands with Charles.

The phone rang. "Yehrr," he said. "Tell the car to wait. I'll be there in five minutes."

Charles went into Adams' office. A chunky, elderly man was sitting on Adams' sofa. It was Al Williams, of the old Stepp Brothers dance team. "Joe, I'm going out a little while. I'll be back in about half an hour," Charles said, and the door closed after him.

Adams sat down behind his desk. It was gleaming and completely bare, except for a couple of pens and a blotter. There was an abstract painting on one wall and photographs of Charles' plane on another.

"In 1959, Ray Charles was going out on the road and he asked me to go with him as the m.c.," Adams said, in his low, manicured voice. "They wanted a little dignity for the show. Then he asked me to go overseas with him. I went. And then he asked me to join him on a personal basis. I agreed. The first six weeks, I never heard a word from him, so I quit. Two weeks later, he sent for me, and I'm still with him. I've never been hired in the sense of a contract. A handshake between gentlemen. Eventually, he started forming his companies, and I now serve as his personal manager and the general manager and vice-president-treasurer of all of them. He's never told me what to do or how to do it. We have the kind of relationship where he's so astute that I should be paying him.

"I was born in Watts when no one had ever heard of Watts. I wanted to take public speaking in school, but they said, 'No, you'll never get a job in radio because you're a Negro.' I used to walk all over Los Angeles looking for work, and some of the people who turned me down are working for me now. I was the first Negro announcer in coast-to-coast radio, and I started with the disc jockey Al Jarvis. I was with N.B.C. ten years, and when I quit I quit at the top, with a Number One rating. It was 1957, and there was no more creativity in the work for me. Along the way, I've worked as a speech-and-diction coach at M-G-M and done a lot of pictures and television shows. I was with Pearl Bailey in *Carmen Jones*. Otto Preminger hired me. And David Merrick put me in *Jamaica* with Lena Horne.

"I design all of Ray Charles' clothing as well as the gowns the Raelets wear. I designed this building, which we built in 1963, and I did all the interior decoration. I'm kind of blessed. I have the good fortune to have good taste. I like things clean and pure. The members of the band have eight changes of uniform and we carry ninety-seven shirts, so that they have a clean shirt every day. When I hire a man for the band I give him an instruction sheet, so he will know how I want him to dress and behave. No drinking on duty, no narcotics, and I will not allow profanity in public. I teach them pride in their work. You can set your watch by the time we start our shows. Once we took a job and were told to hit at eight o'clock. There were only four or five people in the hall. The man who hired us had figured on a half-hour leeway for himself. Well, he begged me to stop the show and I did, but I gave him hell. On the road, I have a road manager and a stage manager and two bandboys, and there are outside people, like seamstresses and tailors. I have learned to fly. During the Second World War, I was with the 99th Fighter Squadron, the first all-Negro squadron, but I washed out. After I had joined Ray Charles, I was always ordering and buying airplane parts, and I wanted to know what they were for, so I took up flying. But I'm a cautious pilot, a scared pilot.

"Ray Charles is a strong man, a remarkable man. He didn't have much help, but he was a millionaire at thirty and he could have quit working a long time ago and been independently wealthy the rest of his life. People never used to think that he could even talk. But he can talk about anything. And he reads a great deal. He sees with his fingers. Once a little piece of equipment had to be replaced in the engine of one of our planes. The mechanics worked five hours on it and couldn't get it properly in place. Ray Charles said, 'Let me see what I can do with that.' In five minutes, he had the job done. He will never compromise himself or his materials. We were sitting in the office of the president of a New York record company once and the man said, 'Ray, I know how you can make a million dollars. Record an album of spirituals.' Charles refused. He felt it was wrong to tamper with religious music that way. He often works from impulse. One night, I was leaving here around eleven, and when I went in to say good night he said, 'Get me a Corvette.' 'I'm sorry,' I said. 'What did you say?' 'Get me a Corvette. That's a car, a Chevrolet, and I want it in gold.' Luckily, I found an all-night automobile dealer who happened to have a gold Corvette. And he used to drive a scooter. There are two Cadillacs sitting out there in the parking lot, but I think he'd rather ride a scooter. I would sit behind him on it and apply pressure to his shoulders to tell him what direction to steer in, and sometimes, on an empty road, we would hit fifty-five. I've seen him go in a strange building and take a flight of stairs three or four steps at a time. If he wants to wear his green tuxedo instead of his black one, he appears in the green one. He tells the difference by finding some little thing on each suit—a loose thread, a button that is a bit off center, a pocket with something different about it. He is a good cook. And he can type seventy words a minute and he plays a good game of chess. He can do more than most people with sight. When we

were making a recording of a tune called 'I Believe' and
the Raelets were held up by bad weather and couldn't make
the session, Ray Charles sang his part and then he sang all
four of the Raelets' parts, in falsetto. It turned out beautifully."

Charles opened the door from his office and stood there
swaying and smiling. "I'm back, Joe." He turned, went into
his office, and, skirting his desk, sat down heavily. "You
know, it's *rainin'* out there. Rains here, and everything
comes to a stop. But it's better than Seattle, which I left in
1950, when I moved permanently to L.A. I'd made my first
records earlier in the year, for a little record company called
Swingtime, run by Jack Lauderdale. We made them with
the McSon Trio. I got an apartment on the west side of
town, and I thought I wanted to stay. Lowell Fulson, who
had the first big hit of 'Every Day,' was here, and Lauderdale thought I ought to go out on the road with him, so I
did, as the added attraction. It was the first time on the road
in my life. We went to Arizona and New Mexico and
Texas. We went out there and tried our best to stay out
there. It was exciting to me. It had a gloss. I stayed with
Fulson a year and a half, and once when we were going
through Texas, Howard Lewis, who was a big promoter
in that part of the country, told Lowell he should have an
agent. He called Billy Shaw in New York, and they arranged a contract. Not long after, we went to the Apollo,
in New York, and the Shaw agency came and heard us and
they signed me and Billy Shaw told me, 'When the day
comes that we don't produce for you, you don't need us.
And when the day comes that you don't produce, we don't
need you.' It sounded cold to me. I was young and enthusiastic, but later, when I got to understand business, I understood what he meant. Lowell began having his problems of
various kinds and I decided I wanted to suffer through my
own problems instead of his. I wouldn't downgrade him.
He was essential to me, and so was Wylie Pitman and
Howard Lewis and Jack Lauderdale and Billy Shaw and the

fine gentlemen at Atlantic Records, where I had my first big hit, in 1954. They were all links in the chain of my success. Shaw booked me as a single attraction, which meant they would send me to a little town and I'd play and sing with whatever musicians was there. I did it a couple of years, but it was hard. It was necessary for me to try and find out what it was like on my own, but playing one-nighters with all those different musicians . . . Man, I *love* music and I hate to hear it played wrong. Early in 1954, I went into a club in Philly and the band was so bad I just went back to my hotel and cried. That band couldn't read and they couldn't hear, either. I called the Shaw agency and told them I couldn't play the job. It was the first time I literally refused to play. They sent someone down to Philly, and the next day we found some musicians and I was able to finish the gig. I needed that job. I didn't have any pocket-ful of money. I couldn't afford to work with that band and I couldn't afford to work without it. But everything happens for a reason, and if it hadn't of been for that ex-perience I might have gone another long while without my own band, because it was a hell of a lot easier to book a single at seventy-five a week than someone with a whole band. I pestered the Shaw people to death and they loaned me the money to buy a station wagon, and I had enough money to make a down payment on a car for myself. I went down to Dallas and put a band together out of people I had heard one place or another. It had Leroy Cooper on baritone, David Newman on tenor, a couple of trumpets—John Hunt and a guy named Bridgewater—and Jimmy Bell on bass. I'd met my second wife, and after I got the band together we were married and moved into an apartment in Dallas. That was a damn good band, and we had our good times and our bad. We were on the road three hundred or three hundred and fifteen days a year, sometimes travelling seven hundred miles one day and a thousand the next, through hot July, or going the two hundred and forty miles between Dallas and Houston on pure ice, at five miles an hour and getting hit anyway by a car and only being forty-five minutes late for our gig. Our first big hit record was 'I Got a Woman,' and then there was 'A Fool for You' and 'What'd I Say' and 'Hallelujah I Love Her So.' My percentage of successes was extremely good. If you can count out seventy-five to twenty-five in your favor, you shouldn't gripe too much. I dearly loved the people at Atlantic. Their engineer, Tommy Dowd, was a marvellous man, and they never told me I had to record *nothing*. They'd submit materials, but I was always my own boss and sometimes I'd send all the tunes back. But this caused me to write my own things, like 'Hallelujah I Love Her So' and 'What'd I Say,' and I did all the arranging for the band. In 1957, when I felt ready to buy a house, my wife and I moved out here. We left Atlantic in 1959 and went with A.B.C. Paramount, where we had our first million-album seller. There were no bad feelings. It was just an honest business arrangement. But I rejoined Atlantic recently. Joe Adams is my executive business manager. He's been with me over ten years. He was a disc jockey with KOWL here and he was very big. Between twelve and three every day, there was no place you could go in Los Angeles and not hear Joe Adams. He first came out on the road with us as an m.c., and I began to study him. He struck me as articulate and very intelligent. He's tight with money and he's got the business where it's manageable. I feel I'm only a small businessman. I'm content to let the business grow as long as I can see a little improvement each year. This is a very slippery business. You have to be careful. It's constantly changing, and you've got to move with it. I remember when there were only a handful of recording companies in the whole country. Now there are I don't know how many.

"I'm not even sure I'm a singer. You certainly need some luck. I've been able to take a pop song, and it paid off, and a country-and-Western, and it paid off, and a blues, and it paid off, and standards like 'Old Man River' and 'Georgia on My Mind,' and they paid off. But I've tried to find songs *I* can get feeling out of. I must please myself first before I sing a song in public. The song must strike me some way in my heart. Now, I love 'Stardust,' but I'll never record it. Every time I sing the song to myself, I can't get the feeling out of it. The same with the national anthem and Nat Cole's 'Nature Boy.' I loved that record, but I can't sing it to sink. But I like to sing 'America the Beautiful.' The lyrics of a song are vital. You become the person the writer is talking about. It's like a dramatic actor. People have come up to me and said, 'That girl Georgia you sing about must have really meant something to you.' Hell, I never had a girl named Georgia, I never *knew* a girl named Georgia. I can be very angry or very sad when I go onstage, but I love music so much I forget that. I refuse to get entangled in something that will make me perform bad. I start to work, it's like a different machine takes over. Tempos are important. I set the tempos, and 'Georgia' may be a hair faster one night or a hair slower the next and it can have a profound difference on the way you sing the words. The melody is your guideline, your radar, but music would mean very little to me if I had to sing it the same way day in and day out. What I do is try and improve on it each time. Change a note here and there, make a twist in your voice, bend a note—take liberties like that. You won't become stagnant if you can change a little each night. I'd have to *make* myself sing the same song the same way twice a year, which some people do every night without any effort at all.

"I can't give any reasons why the public likes me. Of course, one time I might be up and the public might not feel a thing, and another time they might cry and I might consider myself down. The only thing is I have tried to be honest and I cannot be a disappointment to myself. I've felt that way all my life. I've often wondered, Who am I? What am I that people would spend the money to come out and stand in the rain to hear me, come out and spend the money on tickets and baby-sitters and carfare to hear me? But if I can tell myself I did my best, I know in my heart I feel satisfied."

A Quality
That Lets You In

Tony Bennett

The number and variety of American Singers are astonishing and almost endless. Their names form an American mythology: Russ Columbo, Whispering Jack Smith, Gene Austin, Jeanette MacDonald, Nelson Eddy, Sophie Tucker, Alberta Hunter, Arthur Tracy, Al Jolson, Kate Smith, Rudy Vallée, Bessie Smith, Fred Astaire, Louis Armstrong, Mildred Bailey, Red McKenzie, Ivie Anderson, Ethel Waters, Bing Crosby, Ella Fitzgerald, Billie Holiday, Tony Martin, Ethel Merman, Johnny Mercer, Jack Teagarden, Dick Haymes, Josh White, Joe Turner, Jimmy Rushing, Mabel Mercer, the Boswell Sisters, the Andrews Sisters, the Mills Brothers, the Ink Spots, the Golden Gate Quartette, Helen Humes, Mary Martin, Ray Nance, Paul Robeson, Maxine Sullivan, Lee Wiley, Bob Eberly, Ray Eberle, Helen O'Connell, Woody Guthrie, Gene Autry, Pete Seeger, Johnny Cash, Eddy Arnold, Noble Sissle, Richard Dyer-Bennett, Helen Ward, Morton Downey, Martha Tilton, Helen Forrest, Frank Sinatra, Georgia Gibbs, Nat King

Cole, Hoagy Carmichael, Anita O'Day, Kenny Baker, June Christy, Eddie Fisher, Frankie Laine, Vaughn Monroe, Frances Langford, Sylvia Syms, Johnny Mathis, Rosemary Clooney, Leadbelly, Judy Garland, Dinah Shore, Billy Eckstine, Eartha Kitt, Buddy Greco, Peggy Lee, Harry Belafonte, Anita Ellis, Bo Diddley, Elvis Presley, Lena Horne, Doris Day, Pearl Bailey, Perry Como, Margaret Whiting, Mel Tormé, Hugh Shannon, Jo Stafford, Tony Bennett, Blossom Dearie, Teddi King, Mary Mayo, Kay Starr, Patti Page, Carmen McRae, Jackie Cain, Teresa Brewer, Dean Martin, Barbara Lea, Sarah Vaughan, Annie Ross, Ray Charles, Mahalia Jackson, Bobby Short, Helen Merrill, Stella Brooks, Dinah Washington, Chris Connor, Andy Williams, Steve Lawrence, Eydie Gormé, Dionne Warwick, James Brown, B. B. King, Aretha Franklin, Joan Baez, Barbra Streisand, Bob Dylan, Janis Joplin, Nina Simone, Glen Campbell, and Roberta Flack. They have, in the past forty years, become ubiquitous—on the radio, on records, on jukeboxes, in the movies, on the stage, in night clubs, on television, and in concert halls. Indeed, they have created, as a huge, ceaselessly moving and changing body of troubadours, the most pervasive and familiar sounds in American life. Many are famous, and some are among the most famous people of this century. Few adults in the Western world are unaware of Bing Crosby and Frank Sinatra and Judy Garland and Nat King Cole and Tony Bennett and of the anthem status they have, respectively, given such songs as "White Christmas," "I'll Never Smile Again," "Over the Rainbow," "Nature Boy," and "I Left My Heart in San Francisco." One of the reasons for this unique outpouring of song was the invention of the microphone, which, together with its handmaidens, radio and the recording, made two things possible: omnipresent singing, and a successful singing career without a voice. Another was the appearance in the tens and twenties and thirties of the first great American songwriters; the lives of their countless marvellous songs were wholly dependent on being performed, and so a new and insatiable demand for more and better singers arose. Still another reason was our old habit of letting off excess emotional and romantic steam through singing. (Never has there been more singing in this country than during the Depression and the Second World War.) Consider the minstrel singers, the cowboys, the slaves who first sang blues and spirituals, the young women who performed the latest Stephen Foster in the parlor of an evening, the hillbilly singers, the Irish and Neapolitan tenors, and the light-classical singers such as John McCormack and Lawrence Tibbett. The first microphone singers were the crooners, who, with their patent-leather baritones and oily vibratos, evolved from the basically European singing of the McCormacks and Tibbetts in the twenties. And out of the crooners came Bing Crosby, who, cutting the silver cord to Europe, almost by himself invented American popular singing.

Bing Crosby and Ethel Waters were the first American singers to learn this trick, and they did it in large part by listening to jazz musicians. Crosby in particular listened to Louis Armstrong and Duke Ellington (he recorded "St. Louis Blues" with Ellington in 1932), and he was tutored by Mildred Bailey when he was one of Paul Whiteman's Rhythm Boys. He hung out in Chicago with Bix Beiderbecke and Jimmy McPartland. He learned to sing legato, to phrase in a "lazy" fashion. He learned rubato and the ornamental, open-glottal notes—the "aaums" and "oowoos" —that made every phrase he sang sound as if it started with a vowel. The great instrumentalists like Beiderbecke "sing" on their horns, and through them he was taught to flow melodically. He learned to make his comfortable, frontporch baritone appear capacious and important. In turn, he taught a generation of popular singers. The best of them was Frank Sinatra. Sinatra had also listened to Armstrong and Mildred Bailey, but he had, as well, grown up on Billie Holiday and Mabel Mercer. Sinatra was a more serious singer than Crosby. At the outset of his career, Sinatra sang with Tommy Dorsey's band, and Dorsey, a lyrical player of the first order, taught him—in Dorsey's words—how to "drive a ballad." Sinatra's ballads, freed of Crosby's ornamentation and reverberative effects, took on an almost churchlike dimension. He *believed* the lyrics he sang, and he delivered them with an intense, clean articulation. His voice was smaller and lighter than Crosby's, but his phrasing and immaculate sense of timing gave it a poise and stature Crosby's lacked. Sinatra, in his turn, brought along another generation of popular singers, and the best of them is Tony Bennett, who has become the most widely admired American popular singer. Alec Wilder, who has known Bennett for many years, once wrote, "The list of 'believers' isn't very long. But those who are on it are very special people. Among them, certainly, is Tony Bennett. But first I should say what I mean by a believer. He is one whose sights stay high, who makes as few concessions as he can, whose ideals will not permit him to follow false trails or fashions for notoriety's or security's sake, who takes chances, who seeks to convey, by whatever means, his affections and convictions, and who has faith in the power of beauty to survive, no matter how much squalor and ugliness seek to suppress it. I am close enough to him to know that his insistence on maintaining his musical convictions has been far from easy. His effervescent delight in bringing to his audiences the best songs, the best musicians, the best of his singing and showmanship is apparent to anyone who has the good sense to listen to him in person or on records." Wilder went on to ponder Bennett's singing: "There is a quality about it that lets you in. Frank Sinatra's singing mesmerizes you. In fact, it gets so symbolic sometimes that you can't make the relationship with him as a man, even though you may know him. Bennett's professionalism doesn't block you off. It even suggests that maybe you'll see him later at the beer parlor." For all that, Bennett, a ceaseless experimenter, is an elusive singer. He can be a belter who reaches rocking fortissimos. He drives a ballad as intensely and intimately as Sinatra. He can be a lilting, glancing jazz singer. He can be a low-key, searching supper-club performer. But Bennett's voice binds all his vocal selves together. It is pitched slightly higher than

Sinatra's (it was once a tenor, but it has deepened over the years), and it has a rich, expanding quality that is immediately identifiable. It has a joyous quality, a pleased, shouting-within quality. It has, in a modest way, something of the hallelujah strain of Mahalia Jackson.

For a time in the early seventies, before he moved to California, Bennett lived in controlled splendor in a high, spacious apartment on the Upper East Side. At home and on the road, he divided his time between his singing, which is his meat and marrow; tennis, which he had taken up not long before and which he believes is essential to his singing well; drawing and painting, which he has practiced, and commendably, off and on since he was in school; and his family, which included Danny and Daegal, who are grown up, his new wife, Sandy, a cool, pearl-blond, pearl-skinned beauty from Leesville, Louisiana, and their four-year-old daughter, a jumping bean named Joanna.

Bennett lived some of his New York days this way:

MORNING

It was a little after nine, and Bennett, dressed in a silk robe, a yellow shirt, and modish tan pants, walked through his living room and into his studio-dining room. The living room, a careful orchestration of sharp whites, oyster whites, and pale grays, contained a sofa, overstuffed chairs, heavy glass-topped tables, a wall-to-wall shag rug, and a grand piano. A bookcase beside the window held Blake, Picasso, Klimt, Miró, Eisenstaedt, Rodin, Norman Rockwell, Klee, and songbooks by Cole Porter, Jerome Kern, George Gershwin. The studio-dining room was clubbier. Canvases were stacked with their faces to one wall, and above them, on a cork board, were pinned a map of the United States, the Declaration of Independence, and a reproduction of a Bennett cityscape. A big, U-shaped cabinet, covered with paints and brushes, was set against the window, and in front of it, on a slab of Lucite, were a stool and an easel. The longest wall in the room was taken up by a white desk and several shelves of stereo and recording equipment, tapes, albums, books, and framed photographs. A small dining-room table and two chairs were in a corner opposite the kitchen door. Both rooms faced south, and their windows were enormous; standing in the doorway between the rooms, one could pan easily from the Fifty-ninth Street Bridge to the Jersey shore. The sunlight everwhere looked soft and expensive. Bennett turned on an all-music FM station, then stuck his head in the kitchen and asked his cook, Edith, for a mug of coffee. He took a bowl of apples and pears from the coffee table in the living room and put it on a corner of the dining table. A small, new canvas rested on the easel, and after he had squeezed some red, green, and yellow paint onto a palette he started sketching in the outlines of the fruit. The Beatles' "Yesterday" came on the radio, and he hummed along with it. He worked quickly and deftly with his brush, and in a minute or two the outlines of the fruit and bowl were on the canvas. Edith, a trim black woman in a white uniform, put Bennett's coffee on the desk, and he thanked her. He sketched in a vase of long-stemmed red roses on the table just behind the fruit. "I wish I could stop right there," he said, "and just make it a sketch. I always go too far and clutter everything up. It's just recently that I've regimented myself to paint every day. Painting encloses me in a bubble of warmth. When I'm on the road, I take a sketchbook, and it's a relief, between cities, to sketch everything you see. Later, a lot of those sketches turn into paintings." He put down his brush and riffled through a sketchbook lying on the desk. There were scenes of trees and houses in Hollywood, of Eddie Fisher's garden, of a rain-soaked park in Leeds, England, and of chimney pots in Glasgow. They were graphic and tight and detailed. "I don't understand why, but painting comes to me much easier in England. It's almost like I slip into a different style." He picked up his brush and pointed at the reproduction of the cityscape on the cork board. "I'm really pleased about that. It was done right out this window, and the original is in a celebrity art show in Lincoln Center. Red Skelton is in the show, and Kim Novak and Duke Ellington and Henry Fonda. Skelton's painting is of an Emmett Kelly-type clown, which is really a self-portrait. He sold a painting once to Maurice Chevalier, and Chevalier hung it in his house between a Picasso and a Cézanne. Ellington's painting in the show is of Billy Strayhorn, and it's full of flaming blues. It's as mysterious as his music. Henry Fonda's is in the Wyeth school. But I think maybe Kim Novak is the most talented of everybody. She has a beautiful control of paints and a lot of expression. I like Impressionism and the Old Masters—the way Rembrandt could turn out a drawing that was just as fully realized as any painting. I like doing what they did rather than reaching out for something new. I try and paint in their tradition."

Joanna appeared in the living-room doorway. She was about two feet high and had long dark-blond hair and huge eyes. She was in her underwear and held a pacifier in one hand.

"Hey, Jo. How are you this morning, darlin'?" Bennett said.

"Fine. I lost my pink umbrella. It was hanging on my tricycle." Her voice was birdlike.

"Well, we'll look into that. Do you want to sit here on the stool and watch Daddy paint?" He hoisted her onto the stool, and she looked as if she were sitting in a treetop. She dropped her pacifier on the floor, and Bennett picked up an apple from the bowl and handed it to her. She held it in both hands and took a tiny bite. He laughed. "That won't make that much difference. I'll just paint it out." He blended the apple into the background and scraped the results with a palette knife.

"There you are, Joanna," Sandy Bennett said. She was wearing a blue-and-white patterned dress and a blue blazer. Her hair hung over one eye. "Come and get dressed. We have to go and get you some shoes, and then I have to get back here and interview some new nurses." She sighed and pouted. Joanna put down the apple, which had four dime-size bites in it, and skinnied off the stool. "Then I'm going to call the French Lycée, Tony. It might be tough for her, but she can have a tutor, too. There are lycées in Los Angeles and London and Paris, so if we spend three months in any of those places, she'd have a school. I mean, that's what our life style is."

"Right, San," Bennett said, and put the final strokes on his painting. Joanna ran out of the room and Bennett shouted after her, "Hey, Joanna, do you want to go buy a kite tomorrow morning and fly it in the Park?"

"Yes! Whoopee!" she shrieked, and vanished around the corner.

AT THE AMALFI

It was late afternoon on the same day, and Bennett was at a back table on the ground floor of the Amalfi, on East Forty-eighth Street. He had been eating at the Amalfi since the days, twenty and more years before, when it was a one-room place on West Forty-seventh. Phil Rizzuto was a couple of tables away, and Bennett greeted him and sent a drink to his table. Bennett was to sing a couple of songs at ten o'clock at a benefit, and he ordered a light supper of macaroni shells stuffed with ricotta and a bottle of Chianti classico. Bennett has the sort of face that is easily sculptured by light. In broad daytime, he tends to look jagged and awkwardly composed: his generous Roman nose booms and his pale-green eyes become slits. But the subdued lighting in the Amalfi made him handsome and compact. His eyes became melancholy and shone darkly, the deep lines that run past his mouth were stoical, and his nose was regal. His voice, though, never changed. It is a singer's voice—soft, slightly hoarse, and always on the verge of sliding into melody. Rizzuto called over and thanked Bennett for the drink, and Bennett nodded and raised his wineglass in Rizzuto's direction. "I'm not that crazy about singing at big benefits," Bennett said, "but Ed Sullivan, who's running this one, has been good to me and I like him. I like concert halls, and what I do now is pick the best halls here and abroad, and give just one concert on Friday night and one on Saturday. I do that about thirty weekends a year. It's much nicer working concert halls than night clubs. The audience holds on to every inch of intonation and inflection. But night clubs teach performers like me. They teach you spontaneity. They teach you to keep your sense of humor. They teach you to keep your cool. All of which I needed not long ago when I gave a concert in Buffalo and decided to experiment by not using a microphone. The hall isn't that big and they could hear me, but I guess without the microphone I just didn't sound like *me*. So people started shouting. But I remembered what Ben Webster—the great, late Ben Webster—once told me: 'If I had it to do all over again, I'd leave my anger offstage.' And I did. I went backstage and got a mike, and everything was all right. In addition to my concerts, I do television specials, like the one Lena Horne and I did—just the two of us, no one else—a while back. It got very nice notices, which proves you just don't need all those trappings. I also work in Vegas, and at Bill Harrah's places in Lake Tahoe and Reno, for six weeks a year. Vegas is great, with all the performers on one strip, like a kind of super-Fifty-second Street. They can afford anything, and they treat performers marvellously. But Bill Harrah is fabulous. I think he started out with bingo parlors in Reno thirty-five years ago, and now he owns these big places in Tahoe and Reno and has a huge collection of classic cars. He meets you at the airport with a Rolls-Royce and gives you the keys to the car and a beautiful home with a pool. At the end of the engagement, he throws a party for you in his own home. It's like some kind of fantastic vacation."

Bennett took a forkful of shells and a sip of wine. "It's beautiful not to compromise in what you sing, and yet I've done business since I had my first record hit for Columbia, in 1951. I've always tried to do the cream of the popular repertoire and yet remain commercial. Hanging out with good songs is the secret. Songs like 'All the Things You Are' and 'East of the Sun' are just the opposite of singing down. And so are these lyrics, which Alec Wilder wrote and sent me a few days ago. He said if I liked them he'd set them to music. I think they're beautiful." Bennett pulled a sheet of onionskin letter paper out of his pocket. The lyrics read:

GIVE ME THAT WARM FEELING

Give me that warm feeling
That makes me believe again,
Give me that soft answer,
The kind you gave me way back when.
Give me some true kindness
That brightens the sky again.
Give me the best that's in you
And encouragement now and then.
Dust off those long-lost manners!
Bury ambition and guile!
Unfurl those lovely banners
Of virtue and laughter and style!
Give me that warm feeling,
Take off that impersonal glove.
Remember, remember, we're dealing
With that fair and that rare thing called love!

"I love singing too much to cheat the public. And I can't ever lose that spirit by listening to the money boys, the Broadway wise guys who used to tell me, 'If you don't sing such-and-such, you'll end up with a classy reputation and no bread in the bank.' But if I lost that spirit, my feeling for music would run right out the window. It's this obsolescence thing in America, where cars are made to break down and songs written to last two weeks. But good songs last forever, and I've come to learn that there's a whole group out there in the audience who's studying that with me. There's a greatness in an audience when it gets perfectly still. It becomes a beautiful tribal contact, a delicate, poetic thing. A great song does that. It also works two ways: the performer makes the song work, and the song inspires the performer.

"All kinds of things go through my head when I'm singing. I think of Joanna a lot. I think of things from my past; I even *see* them. If I'm working in a beautiful place like Festival Hall, in London, I think of the great lighting, the great clusters of light, and they inspire me. If a song is truly believable, it becomes a self-hypnosis thing. And when that happens I automatically start thinking a line ahead, like when I serve at tennis and am already thinking of the next shot. My concentration becomes heavy, so that if I forget the words I can do what Harold Arlen told me: 'Just make up new words in the right spirit and don't let anybody know, and you'll be all right.'

"I've always liked the Billie Holiday tradition of allowing the musicians you're working with to take charge and to solo, and my arrangements are always written that way. Jazz musicians create great warmth and feeling. When they play well, they make *you* sing, too. I've worked with Bobby Hackett and Woody Herman and Duke Ellington and Stan Kenton and Count Basie. And I've worked with Harry Edison and Jimmy Rowles and Tommy Flanagan and Zoot Sims and John Bunch and Billy Exiner. You can't beat the perfection of Basie. He even talks the way he plays: one or two words take care of conversation for the month. Like when he saw the distance he'd have to go to reach his piano on this tiny, miserable stage we were working on somewhere out West. 'Man, that's a long walk,' he said."

Bennett laughed, and told the waiter, a diminutive carry-over from the old Amalfi, that he didn't have time for espresso but that he would see him soon. He waved to Rizzuto.

KITING IN THE PARK

It was ten-thirty the next morning, and one of those dancing blue New York days: the shadows had knife-edges, and the sidewalks were full of diamonds. Bennett was standing with Joanna at the curb in front of his apartment house. She was holding on to his right index finger, and she barely topped his knees. They were headed for the East Meadow, in Central Park, where a sequence of a quasi-documentary about Bennett's New York life was to be filmed. One sequence had already been done in his apartment, and another would be filmed tomorrow night at a concert he was giving in Alice Tully Hall. Joanna was in a blue knitted jumper with a matching top, and Bennett had on a gleaming white safari suit and a dark-olive shirt open at the neck.

"Daddy, let's go see if the flowers we planted are still growing," Joanna piped.

Bennett hunkered beside some shrubs next to the building's door and rubbed the dirt with his hand. There was nothing there.

"Whynot? Whynot? Whynot?" Joanna chanted.

Bennett looked sheepish. "I guess we forgot to water it, or something. But we'll try again."

A rented black limousine the length of the one Jelly Roll Morton said he had to take to Central Park to turn around pulled up at the curb, and Bennett and Joanna got in. It had a red shag carpet, and the jump seats were separated by a cabinet containing a bar, a radio, and a tiny television set. Bennett told his driver, a squat, cheerful man named Caesar, to stop at a shop specializing in kites, at Second Avenue and Eighty-fourth Street. Two cameramen and a grip followed the limousine in a cab. Joanna diddled with the television, switching from channel to channel, and Bennett told her to slow down or she wouldn't be able to see anything at all. She paid no attention. At the shop, Bennett and one of the cameramen chose a couple of big, semitransparent German kites that looked like birds. Bennett was all thumbs, but he managed to get one of the kites assembled by the time the limousine pulled up at Fifth Avenue and Ninety-eighth Street. The East Meadow stretches from Ninety-seventh to 101st Street and is vaguely bowl-shaped. Joanna sailed in the south gate ahead of Bennett and, sensing the expanse in front of her, took off up the Meadow, her legs going like a sandpiper's. Bennett, laughing and shouting, caught her at 100th Street. The cameramen stationed themselves on a low rise on one side of the Meadow. A time followed that recalled the mad footage in *A Hard Day's Night* in which the Beatles raced wildly and aimlessly back and forth across an immense field. There was almost no wind, but Bennett got the kite twelve feet into the air, and he and Joanna ran up the Meadow. The kite crashed. Joanna picked it up and ran south, Bennett galloping after her. They went up the Meadow, down the Meadow, across the Meadow. Joanna maintained her speed, but Bennett began to puff. The cameramen declared that they had enough film, and Bennett laughed and wiped his brow. He picked up his jacket from the grass and flung it and the kite across one shoulder. Joanna latched on to his index finger and led him back to the car.

A LIGHT LUNCH

Before he showered and changed his clothes at the apartment, Bennett asked Edith to fix a light lunch. Joanna was fed in the kitchen and packed off for a nap. Bennett was due at three o'clock at a studio on Christopher Street, where he was to rehearse with the Ruby Braff-George Barnes Quartet. The quartet was to accompany him at Alice Tully Hall. Edith set the table in the studio and brought in a chicken salad and a large glass of boysenberry juice. "Man, tennis has nothing on that kiteflying," Bennett said. "But all that running around will make me sing better this afternoon. Maybe if I'd known about it a long time ago, it would have gotten my career going a lot faster. The way it was, I didn't become any sort of authoritative singer until I was twenty-seven. For seven years before that, I scuffled. After the war, I used the G.I. Bill to study at the American Theatre Wing, where I worked on bel canto with Peter D'Andrea. And I studied voice with Miriam Speir. It was at her place I first met Alec Wilder. I never passed any au-

ditions, and I worked as an elevator man at the Park Sheraton, in an uncle's grocery store, as a runner for the A.P.,
and as a singing waiter out in Astoria, where I was born. I
was born in August of 1926, as Anthony Dominick Benedetto. I'm using Benedetto again to sign my paintings. We
lived in a little two-story house in Astoria which is still
there. My father came over from Italy in 1922, but I don't
know much about him, because he died when I was nine.
He had a grocery store on Fifty-second Street and Sixth
Avenue, where the C.B.S. Building is now. I remember he
was a beautiful man, who was much loved by his family and
friends. He had an open, warm voice, full of love and melody, and he sang beautifully. He'd always get the family
out on Sundays to sing and dance. My mother, whose
maiden name was Surace, was born down on Mott and Hes-
ter Streets, and she lives out in River Edge, New Jersey.
After my father died, she went to work in the garment dis-
trict and put my brother and sister and me through school.
She has spirit and that great gift of common sense. Judy
Garland went crazy over her when she met her. I went to
P.S. 7 and Junior High School 141, out in Astoria, and then
I went to the High School of Industrial Arts, which used to
be near the Waldorf-Astoria. It was way ahead of its time.
I studied music and painting, and they'd work it so that you
didn't have to be there every day, so long as you did your
work. You could go over to the Park and sketch trees. I
had a music teacher named Sonberg, and he'd bring a Vic-
trola into class and play Art Tatum records. Imagine that!
It was around then I decided to be a singer. Of course, I'd
been singing all my life and in the shadow of show business.
I had an uncle in Astoria who was a hoofer in vaudeville
and worked for the Shuberts. He'd tell me about Harry
Lauder and James Barton and how they were humble people who had their feet on the ground. He'd tell me about
Bill Robinson and how he had to follow him once and it almost killed him. He'd tell me how the acts in those days
honed their shows all the way across the country and back,
so that when they finally got to the Palace in New York

they were sharp and ready. I had my first professional job when I was thirteen, at one of those Saturday-night get-togethers at a Democratic club in Astoria, and later I sang at little clubs by myself when they'd let me." (Harry Celentano, a bellman at the Algonquin, who went to school with Bennett, remembers those days: "He used to sing 'God Bless America' and 'The Star-Spangled Banner' in assemblies, and when he was a little older he'd go into places out there like the Horseshoe Bar and the Queen of Hearts—this quiet, shy little kid—and get up and sing all by himself. Some of us would go with him, and he'd stand there and sing 'Cottage for Sale' like a soft Billy Eckstine. We didn't take him seriously, and we'd shout and throw peanuts at him, but he never batted an eye. But he was also into art then. He would play hooky and draw these huge, beautiful murals right on the street, with chalk. Mothers and children would stop and watch, and they were amazed. Then we'd come along and play football over the mural, and that was that.")

Edith asked Bennett if he'd like more chicken salad, and he shook his head. "My first scrape with any kind of professionalism came at the Shangri-La, in Astoria, where the trombonist Tyree Glenn had a group. He heard me singing along with the band and asked me to come up and do a song. I think it was Duke's 'Solitude.' I'll never forget that kindness. I went into the service late in the war and ended up in the infantry, doing mopping-up operations in France and Germany. My scuffling years began to end in 1949, when I auditioned for a revue Pearl Bailey was in at the old Greenwich Village Inn. It had people like Maurice Rocco, who used to play the piano standing up. I became a production singer in the show, which meant I was a combination m.c. and singer. Pearl told me, 'It'll take you five years before you can handle yourself on a stage, but at least I can get you started.' Bob Hope heard me in the show and asked me to come up and sing at the Paramount Theatre with him. It was his closing night, and before I went on he told me that my stage name, Joe Bari, wasn't any good, and he asked what my real name was. I told him, and he thought a moment and said, 'We'll call you Tony Bennett,' and went out on the stage and introduced me. Then he took me on a ten-day tour with him, and everybody—Les Brown and Marilyn Maxwell were in the troupe, too—showed me how to get on and off the stage without falling down, and things like that. Maybe a year later, Mitch Miller auditioned me at Columbia. I sang 'Boulevard of Broken Dreams,' and it became a semi-hit. This gave me the strength to go out on the road and work clubs in places like Philadelphia and Boston and Cleveland and Buffalo. So I'd started this crazy adventure that has lasted twenty years. Then I had hits like 'Because of You' and 'Just in Time,' and I became international in 1962, when I recorded 'I Left My Heart in San Francisco.' "

Edith came in from the kitchen and said, "The doorman called, Mr. Bennett. The car's downstairs."

THE CONCERT

The concert at Alice Tully the next evening was billed as "An Evening with Rodgers and Hart," and it was a smooth and engaging success. The hall was sold out, and the audience was hip. Bennett sang the verses of most of the songs, and by the time he got a note or two into the chorus there was the applause of recognition. He was in a dinner jacket, and his stage manner was startlingly old-fashioned: he used a hand mike, and he whipped the cord around as though it were a lariat; he half danced, half fell across the stage during rhythm numbers; he saluted the audience and pointed at it. He was clumsy and at the same time delightful. He sang twenty-one Rodgers-and-Hart tunes, and many were memorable. He sang a soft, husky "Blue Moon," and then came a marvellous, muted Ruby Braff solo. "There's a Small Hotel" was even softer, and Braff and George Barnes reacted with pianissimo statements. During Braff's solo in "The Most Beautiful Girl in the World," Bennett sat on a stool to the musician's right, and near the end of "I Wish I

Were in Love Again" he forgot his lyrics and soared over the wreckage with some good mumbo-jumbo and a fine crescendo. "Lover" was ingenious. Bennett sang it softly, at a medium tempo (it is usually done at top speed), then briefly took the tempo up, and went out sotto voce. He did "I Left My Heart in San Francisco" as an encore. The ovation was long and standing.

After a small backstage party, Bennett got into his limousine and was driven home. He settled deep into a corner of the car. "It's what I used to dream of—a concert in a big hall like Alice Tully. But it hasn't all been smoothness since I started doing business. When I had my first record hits, in the early fifties, I suddenly found myself with an entourage, most of them takers. And I didn't like it. Maurice Chevalier was doing a one-man show here around then, and all he had was a piano and a hat, and that made me realize I was off on the wrong foot. Then I've been through a divorce and done a little time on the psychiatrist's couch. But I don't think I need that. Most of the people who go to psychiatrists, their hearts and minds have never caught on to any one desire. I never had that problem. But I had a different one when Frank Sinatra came out in *Life* and said I was the greatest singer around. Sophie Tucker once told me, 'Make sure that helium doesn't hit your brain,' but it did, and for several years, to match up to his praise, I overblew, I oversang. But I've found my groove now. I'm solidifying everything, and working toward my own company. You learn how to hang on to money after a while. I like to live well, but I'm not interested in yachts and fancy cars. There are things I'm searching for, but they won't take a day. I'd like to attain a good, keen intellect. Alec Wilder set one of William Blake's poems to music for me, and I was reading Blake last night. Imagine being that talented and feeling so much at the same time! I'd like to make more movies. I played a press agent in *The Oscar*, and I loved the whole make-believe about it. I'd like my own regular TV show, which would be devoted to good *music*. None of that stuff with the musicians off camera and the shots full of dancers. I like the funny things in this life that could only happen to me now. Once, when I was singing Kurt Weill's 'Lost in the Stars' in the Hollywood Bowl with Basie's band and Buddy Rich on drums, a shooting star went falling through the sky right over my head, and everyone was talking about it, and the next morning the phone rang and it was Ray Charles, who I'd never met, calling from New York. He said 'Hey, Tony, how'd you do that, man?' and hung up."

Moonbeam
Moscowitz

Sylvia Syms

Excellence generally parries neglect with bitterness, stoicism, or a brave and judicious narcissism. Sylvia Syms has long since chosen the last of these weapons. She has said of herself, with her wide smile, "I have no desire to be a superstar. I don't think I could stand the responsibility of having to prove myself every single day. If you don't make it, you have a ball trying. But I've made it. I don't know by whose standards, but I've made it by mine. So the only person I have to satisfy now as far as my singing is concerned is me." She is right, for among students of American singing, she is often spoken of as the counterpart of Frank Sinatra, who, as her indefatigable friend, protector, confidant, and admirer, would agree. During the thirty or so years of her career, she has sung in almost every notable night club in the country. When the night-club business began faltering, in the mid-fifties, she turned to the theatre, where she has appeared on and off Broadway in *Diamond Lil* with Mae West, in innumerable productions of *South*

Pacific, in which she has perfected the part of Bloody Mary, in *Dream Girl* with Judy Holliday, in *Thirteen Daughters* with Don Ameche, in *Funny Girl* with Carol Lawrence, in *Flower Drum Song* and *Camino Real*, and as the lead in *Hello, Dolly!* And along the way she has made recordings, one of which, a daring up-tempo version of "I Could Have Danced All Night," became a hit for Decca in 1956. But time and again, just as she has appeared ready to swim into the lagoon of recognition and financial comfort, she has foundered. The causes have been myriad—an operation; a female rival; her own intransigence toward working conditions, managers and bookers, and clothes; an automobile accident; her physical construction; the twists and turns of her private life; and the tricks of fashion. But she continues to work well as both an actress and a singer. Here is the singer in two different settings—a rehearsal for a concert appearance with the composer Cy Coleman, and sitting-in at The Cookery with her friend Barbara Carroll.

I

It was a sleepy New York Saturday, and Sylvia Syms was in Cy Coleman's sumptuous living room. They were rehearsing a dozen Coleman songs for the concert, which was to take place the next day. She was wearing one of her many djellabahs, and she looked tiny in the high-ceilinged room. She is barely five feet tall, and is plump and shapeless. Her legs, both broken in the accident, look spindly, as does her left arm, which was also broken. Childhood polio has left her with a curvature of the back. But her presence is immediately commanding, and on first meeting her one is surrounded by her rich voice, her frequent laughter, and her rhythmical, dramatic motions. Her moon-shaped face lights up whatever it is aimed at. Her wide mouth is almost always smiling; she has large, slightly slanted eyes, elfin ears, and an aquiline nose; and her broad forehead ends in a helmet of short, coppery hair. She is an impulsive, long-syllabled talker who is apt to sail into any subject *in medias res*, and she did when Coleman excused himself to make a phone call: "Mr. Sinatra sent me his newest single this morning," she said. "I don't know why I call him Mister when I've known him as Francis for so many years. I guess it's my profound respect for him. I don't remember when we first met, but *he* would know. I've watched him greet by name without hesitation someone he hasn't seen in twenty-five years. He's a quiet man, articulate and well-informed, and he's been a gracious friend. When I was in the hospital after my operation, he called every day, or had someone call if he couldn't, and when it became clear I'd need a respirator to take with me wherever I went, he had the best one there is sent to me. I still use it an hour every day. He has a good sense of humor. After my automobile accident, he sent me a pair of skates with the message 'Try these next time,' and I returned the gesture when he opened a tour at Caesars Palace by sending him an antique silver ear trumpet. I've never once watched him sing and not come away with something new. I'm grateful to have been alive during his era. All of which explains why, when I was a guest at his home in Palm Springs and he asked me to sing at some inn we had gone to after dinner, I couldn't. I just couldn't get up there knowingly in front of him and sing. All he said was "Sylvia, you're nuts!' "

Cy Coleman sat down at the piano again and loosed a couple of booming chords. "God!" he said. "The sound of the piano is frightening this early." Sylvia Syms stood in the crook of the piano and put on a pair of granny glasses. They decided on "Witchcraft." By the third measure, her body had begun to reflect her singing. She bounced slowly up and down, rocked her shoulders from side to side, and swung her hips. She has a powerful contralto, but she controls it effortlessly. Her diction is bell-like, but she does all sorts of subtle rhythmic things with the words—sometimes piling them together, sometimes letting them drift. The next number was a slow ballad. Her voice became soft, she stretched out her hands, palms up, and raised her shoulders.

The number was full of crooning turns of phrase, and one heard slow breezes and early stirrings. Then she and Coleman went into a buoyant duet of "Hey, Look Me Over" and a ringing version of "The Best Is Yet To Come," which they did in unison, in harmony, in alternating passages, and as a round.

Sylvia Syms laughed and leaned against the piano. "My! They're going to get a warmed-up lady out at the theatre in New Jersey. What time is it, Cy? I have *no* sense of time and I spend all day at home calling for the time. We have two shows of *South Pacific* today, and they're picking me up at three." Cy Coleman said it was just after one, and he suggested a final rehearsal at noon the next day. Sylvia Syms walked the ten blocks to the small apartment she has long had on Lexington Avenue. She took short steps and swayed from side to side, as if she were shouldering her way through the press of her talk. "For some reason, I got to reminiscing about my childhood with Cy before we started today, and it was painful. I was born the oldest of three children in Manhattan but grew up in Flatbush. My maiden name was Blagman and when I started out I called myself Sylvia Black. Then I saw the name Syms with a 'y' somewhere and I liked it and took it. My mother was a New York girl and so was her mother, but my father came from Russia. It was a great love affair between my father and mother. He yelled a lot at me, but I never heard him yell at her. My mother still lives out there. She's intelligent and funny and articulate, and she still points that finger at us children when we visit her and says do this or do that, but now we just laugh and tell her to jump in the lake. She's very into her Judaism, and I suppose she wishes I were, too. I've always been aware of being a Jewess, but my religion is people. My father designed clothes, and he died when I was seventeen, but I didn't know him as much else than a strict, hardworking family man. I was a very removed child, and it started when I sang with a full and beautiful voice before I'd learned to talk. I sang in my carriage, and later I'd sit on the front stoop and sing at the top of my lungs. But my parents didn't know how to cope with my singing. They were poor and their backgrounds had taught them that the life of a singer or actress led directly to the gutter. My father was sensitive in all areas except the one I was interested in, so I got no help, no formal training. I was born a heavy child, and I grew heavier because I was unhappy. Very soon I created a complete fantasy world. I got a reputation, and I'd hear parents tell their kids to keep away from that crazy Sylvia. I'd stay awake all night listening to music on the radio, and when I was in my mid-teens I started sneaking out of the house after everyone was asleep and going down to New York. I'd get on the subway and go to Fifty-second Street. My father got hysterical when he found out, but that didn't stop me. I had long red coppery-chestnut hair tied in braids and parted in the middle, and I had absolutely no fear of going out in the middle of the night. Who wanted to make passes at a fat Jewish girl from Brooklyn? I became the first of the groupies, and I began learning about the momentary, joyful noises of jazz. And I had the greatest people to teethe on. I got to know Fats Waller. He had bad feet, and I remember him playing the organ in a little church uptown and pumping it with his bare feet. And I got to know Art Tatum. He called me Moonbeam Moscowitz, the Jewish Indian. He'd take me uptown after work to the Log Cabin or Tillman's, where he would play with a tenderness and warmth he never showed downtown. Sometimes Jerry Preston, who owned the Log Cabin, would call my mother and tell her everything was O.K., and around seven or eight in the morning he'd send me home in a limousine. Or else Tatum would take me even further uptown to a grits-and-fried-chicken place, and after we'd eaten we'd walk down the street and watch the sun come up. On my twenty-first birthday, he gave me a little glass piano with his initials on it, but it eventually broke. And three years before he died he had Van Cleef & Arpels make a gold piano with a keyboard of sapphires for the black notes and fresh-water pearls for the white notes. But I don't have that anymore, either. Erroll Garner pestered me about it so much I finally gave it to him, and he took it everywhere, in its original little felt bag.

"Billie Holiday became my mentor, and I copied everything she did, excluding the drugs and booze. She said to me once, 'You know what's wrong with you, Sugar? You love me.' She was a beautiful, dignified lady, with an innate sense of good taste. She was drawn to singing songs you knew she understood. She had a kind of animal relativity to the songs she sang. I have no concept of living within a budget, but once I saved twenty-five dollars and bought her a print gown for her birthday, and she was so pleased you'd have thought I'd given her the moon on a stick. I can remember her in the gown at the Onyx Club, coming down those little stairs in the back and and the lights softening and the room becoming silent and her moving onto the stage and looking just like a panther. She began wearing gardenias in her hair because of me. One night when she was working at Kelly's Stable, she burned her hair with a curling iron just before show time, and I ran down the street to the Three Deuces, where Ada Kurtz had the checkroom. Checkroom girls sold flowers then, and I bought a gardenia and Billie put it in her hair to hide the burned place. Of all the men she married or knew, I think she loved Buck Clayton the most. We were sitting around at the club on the Street where Billy Eckstine had his big band, and B said to Billie, 'Ain't I pretty?' 'Yeh,' she said, 'but you ain't the prettiest.' 'Well, who is the prettiest, then?' B asked her. 'Buck Clayton's the prettiest man in the whole world.' I got to know Lester Young through Billie. In fact, she used to tell me when I started singing that I sounded just like the way he played. He was the first person I ever heard say to his piano player, 'Just play vanilla, man. Just play vanilla,' which meant cut out the embroidery and play the proper chords behind solos. I still use the phrase when I run into an accompanist who thinks he's Niagara Falls. Lester was a quiet, inside-himself man, and he'd always tell me, 'It's hard, Baby, it's hard.' I don't recall how I met Duke Ellington, but he called me Lady Hamilton. He made every woman in the world feel beautiful. Once, when I was working in Chicago, Bentley Stegner, who was a music writer for the *Sun-Times*, took me to hear Duke. It was snowing and blowing and there weren't any cabs, so we walked and walked through knee-deep snow, and I had on an old babushka and my mascara ran all over my face, and when we got there Duke took one look at me and said, 'Lady Hamilton, I don't know where you just came from, but please save a few dried-up bones for me.' I hung out with Mildred Bailey, too. She was a wild lady, and she had a rapier tongue. I'd go to hear her at Café Society, where Barney Josephson would never let me pay, and I went to her little house on Sniffen Court. She was a domestic lady and she loved to eat, and so did I. She thought I looked like her and she'd tell people I was her little sister. She told me I'd be a star but I'd be very unhappy getting there."

Sylvia Syms arrived at her door and pulled a key out of her bag. "Before I moved in here, I lived with the comedienne Pat Carroll in a loft right over the Fifty-fifth Street Playhouse, near Seventh Avenue. When we opened the fridge, film music came out, and we could lie on the floor and look through a little hole and watch the pictures." She put her key in the lock and waved, her stubby fingers spread like a child's.

II

It was eight-thirty on a Monday evening. Sylvia Syms was still in *South Pacific*, but Monday was her day off, and she was in a cab headed for The Cookery, where she was planning to sing with Barbara Carroll. As was her wont, she had spent most of the day at Elizabeth Arden getting the week's accumulation of "Texas dirt" she used for makeup as Bloody Mary removed from her face and arms. She was wearing a beautiful black-and-white cotton knit suit, and her hair was arranged tightly around her face and she looked radiant. She leaned into a corner of the seat, and her legs lifted from the floor. "I met my great friend Barbara in 1946. I'm not a woman's woman, and Barbara and Judy Holliday and Pat Carroll have been my only women friends. When I first met Barbara, it was like seeing my reflection in a mirror. We've been through just about everything together, including the automobile accident. I was about to go back to California to audition for the mother in the television series *Bridget Loves Bernie,* and I'd been visiting Barbara at her country place in South Salem. We were being driven back to New York in her little car, and Barbara insisted she sit in the front, so I got in the back with her daughter, Susie. We were coming to a toll gate and Susie and I were playing some kind of game, and the brakes failed and—whammo! I threw myself on top of Susie and she was unhurt. Barbara looks as beautiful as ever, but I don't know how many operations she's had on her face. I was in and out of a wheelchair for a year and a half. But, please God, I'm in fine shape now. I consider that I've come through smelling like a rose, which is why I spend every available minute finding out what the rest of the garden is like."

At The Cookery, Barney Josephson embraced Sylvia Syms, and asked her when she was coming to work for him full time. She told him that he couldn't afford her but that she would work for him at scale. He gave his Ed Wynn giggle and shook his head and seated her near the piano. Barbara Carroll finished her set, and she and Sylvia embraced. Barbara asked her if she would sing during the next set, and Sylvia said yes. Sylvia examined her face in her compact mirror. "It doesn't matter if I'm Sarah Schlepp during the day. But when I perform I have to wear the best. As a result, I've turned into a not-half-bad-looking woman. In the broadest sense, I like me. I even enjoy the things about me I'm not too crazy about. But I didn't feel that way during my first singing job, which was at Kelly's Stable. I went in there one night with a couple of Brooklyn friends and auditioned with Benny Carter's group for Ralph Watkins, the owner, and he offered me a job for the summer. I'd met dear

Benny one night at Nick's, and his daughter and I hung out a lot. It was 1940, and Ralph Watkins paid me twenty-five dollars a week. The Nat Cole Trio was the intermission group and Billy Daniels was the star. The job worked out O.K., but I didn't have the right clothes and I must have looked awful. I didn't work again for five years, and then I went downtown into the Little Casino. I was there a whole year, and Ram Ramirez, who composed 'Lover Man,' was my accompanist. Mike Levin wrote about me in *Down Beat,* comparing me with Billie Holiday and Lee Wiley. I was a buxom, sharp broad, but I was stupid enough to resent the comparisons. I guess I thought I was Topsy and had just grown all by myself. But on the strength of the piece I was hired at the Club Troubador for two hundred dollars a week. Louis Jordan and his Tympany Five were there, and so was Georgie Auld's big band. Another singer, who shall remain nameless, was starred. Well, I was breaking it up, and she wasn't, and one night after work Mike Colucci, who ran the place and was a nice gent, told me, 'Sylvia, I have to fire you.' He wouldn't tell me why, and I was crushed. I found out later what had happened. The other singer's manager handled all sorts of big acts, like Nat Cole and Stan Kenton, and when he heard I was hurting his act he called Colucci and said, 'Get rid of Sylvia Syms.' In the fifties, when I was working in New York, this great big man came in to hear me five nights in a row, and finally he introduced himself and told me I was the best singer he'd ever heard. It was the same gent who had had me fired, and I was flabbergasted. All I could say was 'Oh yeah, how come you did what you did to me at the Troubador?' and all he said was 'She was my act and you were killing her. If you had been my act and someone else was killing you, I'd have protected you in the same way.' I had a gossamer vision of the business. I romanticized it, and I guess in some ways I still do.

"In 1946, I got married for the first time. Actors have always been my downfall, and I married Bret Morrison, who was doing *The Shadow* on radio. He's one of the nicest men I've ever known, and he's probably the only man I'd marry if I ever married again. Anyway, I was a rotten wife. I had my head in too many places. We lived in an elegant duplex on West Sixty-seventh Street, but it was a mausoleum, and it turned me off. We had all the right linen, the right china, the right crystal—and all the wrong ingredients for a good marriage. We were together until 1953. In the mid-fifties, I married Ed Begley—the dancer, not the actor— but it's not a part of my life I like thinking about.

"My being fired at the Troubador gave me a mysterious quality. It was O.K. to be fat if you were exotic. I have some pictures of myself from the mid-fifties when I reached two hundred and forty-two pounds. I looked Chinese. People didn't know what to make of me, and because of my dark complexion they started asking me if I was black. In fact, a lady television interviewer asked me the same question a while ago. I started working in every upholstered joint in New York, and I began to create a nice following. I was in the Ruban Bleu in 1951 with the Norman Paris Trio, and I worked off and on for several years at the Village Vanguard. People like Orson Bean and Robert Clary and Harry Belafonte came and went there, but I stayed on forever. I worked at the Show Spot with Barbara when Mabel Mercer was upstairs in the Byline Room. But I have always been just another name on the lists of the various managers who have handled me—mostly, I think, because they haven't known what to do with me. I even had one once who told me I should be grateful I was working because I was such a mess, which did its little damage. I was never good-enough-looking to sing with a band, and in a lot of the rooms I worked you were required to mix with the patrons, and I just didn't know how. But in 1954 the managers Pete Cameron and Monte Kay came into my life, and they got me a recording contract with Decca. Nothing much happened until 1956, when, at the end of a session, Milt Gabler, who was the A. & R. man, reluctantly let me record 'I Could Have Danced All Night.' Reluctantly! They were dead set against it. Rosemary Clooney had had a hit version on Columbia for a couple of months, and on top of that I wanted to do it at double tempo, which nobody had done. But a month later my version took off and became a hit, and so did other tunes I recorded, like 'In Times Like These,' 'Dancing Chandelier,' and 'It's Good to Be Alive.' The upshot was I got job offers all around the country in hotels and night clubs, and it nearly destroyed me. They expected Miss America but they got me. I still didn't know how to dress, and the clothes I wore made me look like the 'Beer Barrel Polka.' It got so if Ed Sullivan wanted someone to sing 'I Could Have Danced All Night' on his show, he asked Julie Andrews and not me. But I've finally discovered that your wardrobe can be one of your most important assets. There are women in every audience who spend the first twenty minutes of a singer's performance counting the sequins on her dress."

Barbara Carroll stopped at the table and said she'd play a few numbers before Sylvia Syms sang. After she had run through five or six, she smiled at Sylvia and announced her. Barbara moved to the far end of the piano bench, and Sylvia sat down beside her. They looked like girls sharing a swing. Sylvia warmed up with Sammy Cahn's "Can't You Just See Yourself?" She smiled broadly, lifted her head, and slowly rotated her shoulders. When the number was over, she eased into Harold Arlen's "As Long As I Live." Her head bounced up and down, and she snapped the fingers of one hand. She moved right inside the song, and, heating up the words, poured them out through the runnel of the melody. Then she sang an exquisite version of Billie Holiday's "Easy Living," and that created a peculiar sensation. The way Billie sang the song ran along behind her, and the two seemed to be singing a duet. She moved with a deliberate, almost heavy ease from word to word, and her voice echoed off Billie's. She finished, and, crossing one knee over the other, folded her hands on her raised knee. Her voice dropped into a low buzz, and in a gentle, staccato fashion out came the opening words of "Imagination." The staccato passage eased away, and Sylvia went into a legato bridge. The deceptive ease with which she sang made her softest phrases ring. She considered herself a narrative singer, a storyteller who happened to sing her stories, and it was easy to see why. The room was in thrall and when she was done there was a long moment before the applause. She stood, bobbed quickly several times, and returned to the table. Barbara Carroll laughed and clapped; the swing had stopped.

Sylvia Syms looked in her mirror, and ordered more coffee. People came over to the table and told her how beautiful she sounded, and she replied with a round of pleased "Thank you, darling"s. "Being a performer is like suffering a chronic condition," she said after they had gone. "Performing is also the most dominating mistress in the world; I'd never have been able to give so much to a human being. Singing for me is my total cleansing. It's what keeps Mabel Mercer young and full of the gorgeous juices and adrenalin, and it does the same for me. I have to have a personal, almost physical relationship to the songs I sing, so I paraphrase them in my head for my own understanding. I can't sing 'The Boy Next Door,' nor can I sing Cy Coleman's 'Big Spender,' because it's about a prostitute. And I don't understand singers who make a swinging thing out of a tragic song like 'Love for Sale.' So lyrics are terribly important to me. My notes follow the words and they generally land in the right places, but if they don't I invariably know it. If you laugh when you're singing, an audience will laugh with you, but if you cry, the audience won't cry with you. That is Mr. Sinatra's secret: his joy, his emotion never overreach; they always stop just in time. There has to be a certain amount of improvisation in my singing. I almost always breathe a song in the same way, but the notes are given a different emphasis. I perform in a one-to-one way. I have to *see* a face in the audience, and then I'll sing to that face. It's a very personal thing, to sing *to* people and not at them. I *need* my audience, which is why I never sing to myself at home.

"Before I leave for the great beyond, I'd like to do an album of all the songs I've done before, the songs I did first and kind of feel I own. I'd like Gordon Jenkins and Don

Costa to do the arrangements, and I'd sing Sammy Cahn's 'Guess I'll Hang My Tears Out To Dry' and Harold Arlen's 'As Long As I Live.' And there'd be James Shelton's 'I'm the Girl' and his 'Lilac Wine,' which only singers like me sing. And I'd do 'Mountain Greenery' and 'Imagination' and all the Jimmy Van Heusen and Rodgers-and-Hart songs I've done before. I'd call the album 'On Second Thought.' I think it would be an important thing. When you ask as much as I have of this world, you have to leave something in exchange."

According to
Where I Go

Hugh Shannon

There are four consummate cabaret singers in this country:
Mabel Mercer (Staffordshire, England; 1900), Bobby Short
(Danville, Illinois; 1924), Blossom Dearie (East Durham,
New York; 1926), and Hugh Shannon (De Soto, Missouri;
1921). Their bearing, style, voice, and attack are totally
dissimilar, but their repertoires overlap, and they are in the
same line of work—singing superior songs, some of them
largely unknown, to small audiences in intimate rooms in
such a way that song, singer, listener, and room become
one. Mabel Mercer is their doyenne. There is no gifted
American singer who has not learned from her. She came
up through English vaudeville and the Paris boîtes—in particular, Bricktop's—and settled here in 1941. She studied
singing for a time, and she approaches each song as if she
were introducing it: here are its lyrics, my dears, here is its
melody, and here is the beautiful whole they make. She sits
almost motionless in an armchair when she sings (or sing-
talks, depending on her powers that evening), her head

tipped back, her hands occasionally sketching air, her eyes fixed on the middle distance. Her regal bearing goes Queen Elizabeth one better: Mabel Mercer has humor. She alone of the four does not accompany herself. Sometimes Bobby Short's elegance appears brittle and baked-on, but it is not, for his taste—clothes, songs, witticisms—is infallible. He declaims his songs, and he occasionally ends them with an arms-wide, lights-out, bass-drum-thump theatricality. His diction peals, and he has enormous energy. Like Mabel Mercer, he is black, and his accent, a fastidious drawl, both mocks and celebrates his listeners. His piano playing tends to race around, upsetting tempos and dynamics, but he knows the right chords, and once in a while he achieves an Art Tatum fleetness. He grew up close to jazz. So did Blossom Dearie, who is short and blond and has a buttermilk attractiveness. Her little, high voice suggests thimbles and Limoges. Her diction is crystalline, and she is a precisionist; once she has a song set, she never changes a note or a nuance. She also demands silence when she performs. Of these four singers, she is the only one who writes songs. They are funny, light, and highly melodic. She plays the piano like Nat Cole, and she swings. Hugh Shannon is perhaps the least well known of the four. He has spent much of his career in Capri and Paris and Rome and the Virgin Islands. His admirers include some of the wealthiest people in the world, but he considers himself a "saloon" singer. He has a hoarse, rangy baritone, and he flings his songs out. His singing is cheerful and full of bonhomie, and, unlike Mercer and Short and Dearie, who keep their audiences at arm's length, he gathers his listeners to him. His diction is good but loose, and he addresses the piano as if it were sliding past him; he sits ajar, his left foot banging the floor and his hands making fast, pawing motions. He talks to his songs. He will finish a ruminative "Poor Butterfly" and say softly, in a sort of coda, "Poor girl, poor girl." A typical Shannon set includes Cole Porter's "I Get a Kick Out of You"; Rodgers and Hart's "Disgustingly Rich"; Porter's mysterious "Down in the Depths on the Ninetieth Floor"; Stephen Sondheim's

"Send in the Clowns," perhaps the first popular anthem since Harold Arlen's "Blues in the Night"; Herman Hupfeld's "As Time Goes By," complete with a Louis Armstrong epilogue, in which he chants the title three times; Porter's funny "The Great Indoors"; Hoagy Carmichael's "Baltimore Oriole"; Noël Coward's "A Room with a View"; "Poor Butterfly," which is by Raymond Hubbell; and Porter's "Ace in the Hole."

Shannon is a trim, handsome man with sandy hair and a square, unsoft, lined Irish face. He has a brilliant, lopsided smile. When he is in New York, he shares an apartment with the publicist Gus Ober. It is in the East Seventies and looks out over the river from the twenty-fourth floor. Its small living room has a baby grand, bric-a-brac, oils, chinoiserie, a typewriter, gold draperies, and parquet floors, and it opens onto a vertiginous balcony that holds a wrought-iron table and four wrought-iron chairs. Shannon sat in his living room not long ago and talked. He talks very fast, sometimes gaining so much momentum that his words lock, blur, and become unintelligible. At one point, he talked for a solid hour. He sipped white wine, and, like Gertrude Stein, who felt that great views should be ignored to be appreciated, he sat with his back to the river. He is something of a dandy, and he was wearing a white lace shirt, a gold necklace laden with big gold coins, two-toned blue jeans, and red Moroccan slippers. This is what he said:

"Billie Holiday was my idol when I first came to New York, right after the Second World War. Meeting her changed my life. I was going with Marjorie Merwin, who admired Billie as much as I did, and Marjorie's mother would give me hundred-dollar bills. We'd go to the Downbeat Club, on Fifty-second Street, and I'd be so underfoot that Billie couldn't miss me. It got so she'd ask me to hold her dog, Mister, while she sang. One night, I persuaded her to go to a party Inez Cavanaugh was giving for Duke Ellington. She didn't want to, because she knew she'd be asked to sing. When she was, she said, 'If the kid will play for me.'

After she'd finished, Inez made *me* sing. Well, I'd only worked weekends at college as a singer and pianist, but I did, and Billie said, 'Man, you don't sound like nobody! You *gotta* sing!' I could have burst. I was supposed to go into advertising, but instead I went to Provincetown for the summer of 1946. A whole bunch of us took a house in the dunes. It was miles from anywhere, and it had a hot plate and an outdoor shower. Marlon Brando and Joy Cabot and Sydney Shaw and a radio actor came. Brando was not known yet, but he'd got good reviews in a show called *Truckline Café,* which lasted about ten days. I found a job almost immediately playing in a Portuguese bar that had a Bechstein upright. Gradually people knew I was there and started coming in, and it became almost chic. Then Julius Monk arrived in Provincetown with Imogene Coca and Daphne Hellman, and we did shows on Sunday nights in a room in the old Atlantic House. The ladies wore evening gowns—I think the Provincetown people thought they were nightgowns—and we filled the place. Maybe that's why we were raided out at our shack. I came home from work one night and Sydney Shaw was making tea and Marlon was playing his bongos and absolutely nothing was going on, when there was a rap at the door and there were the police. We were charged with disturbing the peace, and there was a hearing. The room was jammed and people were even leaning in the windows. The judge would ask, 'Where do you all sleep?' and we'd say, 'We have two pallets,' and he'd ask, 'How do you sleep on two pallets?' and we'd answer, 'It depends on who gets home first,' and so on. When the judge questioned him, Marlon got surly. In fact, he gave one of his better surly performances, and it all ended with our paying ten-dollar fines. Marlon used to accuse me of snobbishness, because I wore a dinner jacket when I worked. I told him he was a reverse snob, because he was always scratching and snuffling. But we did build a marvellous sand castle together.

"That summer, I met a girl from *Vogue* who had a wonderful apartment overlooking the Washington Square Arch, and when I got back to the city I bought a piano for eighty-five dollars and moved in. Ram Ramirez used to come up and there were always lots of Katherine Dunham's girls around. Julius Monk wanted me in Ruban Bleu, but I wasn't ready. I took a warmup job at a place in Jackson Heights, Queens, called the Blue Haven. We went back to Provincetown for the summer and Chemtoned the room in the Atlantic House dark blue and green and white, and we called it the Atlantic House Cabaret. Julius and I played two-piano duets, and Daphne Hellman had her harp and Schiaparelli gowns. Stella Brooks taught me 'West End Blues,' and Eileen Cook and Bibi Osterwald were there. Julius had a birthday party, and Stella Brooks banged Tennessee Williams' boyfriend's head against the wall. In the fall, I took another job in Queens, at the 22 Club, in Woodside. I alternated with a band every twenty minutes, but I had plenty of time to get my tunes together. My first fan was a bus driver who'd park his bus outside the door every night and come in to hear me. After a while, the New York crowd, led by Faye Emerson and Elliott Roosevelt, showed up. I stayed at the 22 until January, when I went to Key West. Julius called and hired me for Le Perroquet, a new club on Second Avenue. In the fall, Stella Brooks came to Perroquet, too. She was most of all amusing, and she was a past-master of trivia. Truman Capote was so crazy about her —I think he was fascinated by her rudeness—that he took an apartment over Perroquet to be near her. He decorated it all in black. *Every*thing was black but him. One late night, I ended up sleeping on the floor there, and when I woke up I thought, My God, I'm dead. There was no light. Nothing. Cy Coleman, who was very shy, came to Perroquet that winter and alternated with me. Then I went to the Empress Room, which had been opened for me, and Johnny Guarnieri was the other pianist. He loved to smoke cigars, and he wasn't used to Upper East Side supper-club types. By this time, I'd moved to the East Sixties, and I'd become a friend of Peggy Fears. She was a former Ziegfeld girl who'd married A. C. Blumenthal, who owned lots of theatres.

Peggy gave five-o'clock soirées. Tallulah and Joan Bennett and Joan Crawford came when they were in town. Peggy'd been in New York when Lindbergh came back from France; she was always in the right place at the right time.

"One night at the Empress Room when I was playing 'Ballin' the Jack,' a voice said, 'Stop that tune!' It was Bricktop. I'd read about Bricktop everywhere—in Waugh and Fitzgerald—but no one had ever said whether Bricktop was a man or a woman. She came up and sang 'Ballin' the Jack' with me, and then we did a blues, a madeup blues. She was on her way from Mexico to Paris, and she told me she was going to take me with her as her new discovery. She was looking for a place to open a club, and I think Schiaparelli and Donald Bloomingdale were behind her. Julius Monk also wanted me for a place he planned to open in the South of France, and Peggy Fears wanted me to come over to Carrère, in Paris. I said yes to everybody, and I've since learned that that is what you must do to keep going in the saloon business: if you accept two or three jobs, one invariably works out. I had a little Pepsi-Cola stock and I sold that and went over on the Vulcania in steerage in a cabin with about eighteen other people. But I had my dinner jacket. When I passed up from the bowels of the ship into first class, I was properly dressed. We landed in Naples, and I took a fruit boat to Capri. It was unbelievable—villas perched like flowers on the rocks, which looked like sea horses, villas perched in the sky over the sea. I went to work in Numero Due. It was in an old wine cellar and had a beautiful grand piano, and I was an immediate success. They hadn't heard any American music for years, because of the war. Mussolini's daughter used to come in. She was very severe, and sometimes she stayed a short while and sometimes she stayed for hours. I finally found out she only liked one song I did— 'Big Wide Wonderful World'—and when I'd done it she'd leave. I thought the whole situation was a lark, and had no idea I'd spend six or seven seasons there. So I quit in the middle of August, which was extremely bad form, and went to Cap d'Antibes. I had always travelled with letters of recommendation, and I had letters to Elsa Maxwell and Peggy Bainbridge. The bar in the Hôtel du Cap had a place for me for the rest of the season. Then I went to Paris, and Peggy Fears arrived and the five-o'clock soirées resumed. Carrère, which was done in yellow and white and was frighteningly chic, hired me. Doris Duke was back with Ruby Rubirosa, and I taught her to play blues on the piano. She had a light touch, like most women, and she was loaded with determination. I went to Montmartre one night and on the way back was in an enormous car crash and ended up in the hospital with twenty-seven stitches and a split front tooth. Someone sent a case of champagne, and the soirées moved to the hospital. I didn't want to go back into Carrère with my split tooth, so I hid in a tiny place, the Mars, where I was paid nine lavish dollars a night. I was practically anonymous at first, then everybody materialized—the Dunhams and Josephine Premice and Kitty Kitt and Brickie. They were in every night. If amusing people like each other, they'll see each other the next night and the next. That spring, Brickie opened a place in Montmartre with two pianos and a Chinese cook. There were limousines everywhere on opening night. The Windsors came, and Rosita Winston and Doris and Ruby, and it went on until eight in the morning, and soon Brick had put every other place like it out of business. It was divinely dark inside, but that didn't mean I could forget my manners—manners that have become ironclad. I never let on if I forget a name, because I never forget a face, and names invariably come back to me within three minutes. And I never move forward first when I greet someone. I wait for them to move. I went back to Numero Due the next season. Then back to Paris and on to London for the first time, where I sang in the International Club. I had some suits made and acquired a taste for oysters, which is what you do in England. And I met Betty Dodero. I had seen her yacht from afar that summer. She had just got a divorce from Alberto Dodero, who was an immensely wealthy Argentinian. She was Eva Perón's best friend. That winter, I took off for St. Thomas in the Virgin Islands, and became the first supper-club singer there. I had another season in Capri and for a short time was in Toni's Caprice in New York. It was all black and white, and it was quite stunning—one of the most beautiful rooms I've ever worked. They finally had to build bleachers behind the piano and cover them with cushions to handle the overflow. Betty Dodero appeared the next year in the islands. She would sit next to me all night and fan me while I played. We fell in love. She was Swedish and Irish and beautiful, and she had a marvellous sense of humor. And she never forgot a lyric. We lived together, and Betty never left me. We carried Benchley and Waugh and Dorothy Parker and Wodehouse everywhere, and Betty read them to me, over and over. She had a wonderful voice. Capri was magnificent that summer. Bea Lillie, Noël Coward—he and I playing four-handed piano—Judy Garland, Lena Horne, Ella Logan, Sophie Tucker, Gracie Fields, Patrice Munsel. One night, most of them appeared at once and they performed. It was the richest night of my life.

"I had already told Betty: You're very rich. You're very beautiful. You have everything I ever wanted. I love you. But I want *you* to tell me when we should get married. She finally did, and we had a civil ceremony in December of 1952, in New York. We were content. We needed no one else. Our lives took on a pattern for the next five years—the islands in the winter, Capri in the summer, and occasional jobs in New York and Nassau. Then the Germans discovered Capri, and it lost its chic. I worked part of the summer of 1957 in Westhampton, and it was my first time in the Hamptons. Henry and Anne Ford and the Southampton crowd came, as well as the Capri and Paris people. It is not braggadocio to say that I was becoming—indeed, have become—a kind of movable feast, a catalyst. People make their summer and winter plans according to where I go. Everybody has to go someplace, and they know that they will be safe where I am—that they will see their old friends, and that they will meet the right new people. Of course, it works both ways: I'm as happy to see them as they are to see me.

But you must make the audience more important than yourself. When you outgrow your audience, or think you have, you're in trouble. In 1957, Betty began feeling unwell, and in January, 1959, we found out she had cancer. She was operated on and treated for six months. She had no pain. We were very quiet. We spent our last night watching TV. I think it was a 'Late Late Show.' I fell asleep, and when I woke Betty was gone. Patrice Munsel and her husband came and took care of me, and I lived with them a year. Julius Monk kept after me to go back to work, and finally I did, at Downstairs at the Upstairs, which was like working in Grand Central Station. Rose Murphy, who was there for a while, taught me that the way to handle noisy people is to look right at the spotlight and sing to it. That way, you look as if you knew something they didn't, and they quiet down in order to find out. I went to Rome—to Bricktop's on the Via Veneto—in the summer of 1960, and then to a villa in Stresa. I wrote a musical based on Betty's life, and it was terrible. And I wrote a sort of autobiography, which isn't too bad. I discovered I'm not a writer, and I rediscovered that I love playing the piano and singing more than anything else in the world.

"I don't know how many songs I know, but it must be in the thousands. I can immediately sing a song I haven't touched in twenty years. When I put my hands on the keyboard, it becomes a muscular chain reaction. The hands, the head, the voice—they all work together, and up come songs I thought I'd forgotten or didn't know I knew. There are certain tunes I don't like and will not sing, such as 'The Lady Is a Tramp' and 'Ebb Tide' and 'Tenderly.' 'My Ship' is a woman's song, and so is 'Love for Sale.' But I will sing songs that Mabel Mercer and Bobby Short won't touch— things from the Top Forty. My people request them because they want me to think they are with it. I never want anyone to leave when I'm playing—that goes back to my childhood—so I try to make my audience happy even if it kills me, and sometimes it almost does. Occasionally, I will sing four or five straight hours, and it takes something to keep control of myself. One July 4th at the Sea Spray, in East Hampton, I played without stopping from ten in the evening until three in the morning. The place had been doing a poor business until then, and suddenly hundreds of people arrived, so I played and played and played. If you are fair to the house, the house will be fair to you. It was a roasting night and the perspiration poured down my nose and fell on my feet, which were bare, because I always play in bare feet in the summer, and the only way I kept going was by thinking, I'm getting thin, I'm getting thin, I'm getting thin. A lot of my people come in every night, and they become mesmerized. They begin to think they *own* me. They study every expression, every wrinkle. Then they tell me later they know I'm not feeling well when I'm feeling perfectly fine, or they tell me I look extremely happy when actually I'm miserable.

"When a tune has really become mine, I move around inside my head while I sing. I think brilliant thoughts, I think of places I've been and people I've known. I go to 470 Park Avenue, where Betty and I lived, or to Numero Due in Capri, and no one watching me has the least idea where I am or what I'm up to. I hear Betty reading Benchley or 'Vile Bodies' again. Sometimes I even go back to De Soto, where I was born. It's thirty miles outside of St. Louis, and it had a population of five thousand. It was built on seven hills, like Rome, and it had a creek going right through the middle of it. I'm exceedingly grateful to have been born and raised in a small town. How dreadful to be brought up in a city, thinking that people are evil! In a small town, you learn about friends and you learn about snobs. You learn stability and a sense of decorum and discipline. I went to church four times on Sunday, and I was taught not to speak until spoken to, which is why I talk so much now. I was raised by my maternal grandparents, whose name was Stall. My mother died when I was born, and my father, who was just nineteen, deposited me with my grandparents when I was nine days old. I saw him only twice after that, but I don't blame him for what he did. How could a nineteen-year-old boy raise a baby? My grandmother, whom I called Mother, was a calm, strong, dignified woman. She taught me so well to be independent that I became a nonconformist. She always said two things: Play tennis with people who are better than you are, and never travel without a dinner jacket. I don't play tennis anymore, but I prefer being around people who are smarter than I am. My grandfather was one-quarter Sioux Indian, and he was very good to me. He was a conductor on the Missouri Pacific, and he grew roses. People came from miles away to see his roses. We had the first tennis court in town. My uncles built it themselves, and my grandfather put up chicken wire around it. When I got old enough, I raked it and watered it and rolled it. We did not have a lot of money, but we had a big house, with three floors and one bathroom. We used to sit on the porch summer nights with the crickets going, and people always stopped by and talked. Sometimes they told ghostly stories in that wonderful Missouri twang—stories that would make your spine ripple on a dark summer night, with the heat lightning behind the trees and the breeze beginning to smarten. I started taking voice lessons when I was five, from a Mme. Centorbi, and I also started piano lessons with Mme. Theobald. They were both very grand. I studied piano until I was seventeen, but all the while I went down to the sheet-music store and I learned every new tune that came out. I had a marvellous speech teacher, Martha Mae Boyer, who chose all the books I read—*War and Peace* and Thomas Wolfe and Benchley and Fitzgerald—and when I graduated from high school as valedictorian, she helped me get two scholarships to the University of Southern California. My grandparents wanted me to go to a Methodist college for a year and then to Yale, but I wanted to go where the pretty people were, where the convertibles and the blondes were. My grandmother was surprised when I told her, but no one ever raised a voice in our house, and I think she was even a little proud of my determination—even though she was never pleased at my becoming a saloon singer and hobnobbing with Roosevelts. I took the Missouri Pacific out and got a job in a boarding house owned by a woman who treated me like a slavey. I served breakfast and dinner and cleaned up, ironed her two sons' shirts, and slept on a couch in the living room. But soon I moved into a house with a couple of classmates, and pledged Sigma Nu, and was the campus representative for Phelps-Terkel's clothing store— that meant wearing their clothes and being in the shop every afternoon, which was fine, because I already loved clothes. Then Joe Barbados and I opened a club just for students. We called it Barbados, and I played there every Friday and Saturday. I majored in advertising and merchandising and graduated in the top ten in 1941, and then worked as a movie extra. I joined the Navy, and they sent me to Harvard for six months. I went to dances at Pine Manor, where all the girls wore black lipstick, black nail polish, and black velvet. I asked for the Seabees when I finished Harvard, because I couldn't stand the stuffies I'd been with there, and it was the best thing that ever happened to me. I was in the 119th Battalion, Edwin C. Mackay commanding. I think he'd only gone through seventh grade, but he was brilliant. I became disbursing officer, which meant handling the payroll, and I was put in charge of the Officers' Club. The first thing I did was buy a piano, and we took it everywhere. We were sent to New Guinea, where we did a lot of waiting. I wrote letters and read *The Magic Mountain* twice. My God! Settembrini and Peeperkorn and the rest—how well I knew them! At night, everybody got drunk. I controlled all the liquor, and had I wished to I could have made two hundred dollars a bottle. An officer in my battalion was alcoholic, and one night he set fire to my mosquito netting with me inside because I wouldn't let him have booze when he wanted it. I'm crazy about Christmas, and I had brought four sets of Christmas-tree lights with me to the South Pacific. At Christmas, the Seabees raised a huge pole in which they had drilled holes and put branches from whatever trees were available, and I hung my lights, and we had a beautiful tree. Then we were sent to the Philippines.

One Sunday, I went to a Catholic church and a local boy
was playing a huge bamboo organ that the Seabees had put
back in working order. It had a reedy, flutelike sound, and
no bottom. The boy seemed to know only one song, and it
was terribly familiar, but I couldn't place it. Then I got it.
It was 'Don't Get Around Much Anymore' done as a dirge.
When the war ended, all fifteen hundred of us took off our
clothes and stayed drunk two days. In the middle of
this, it suddenly came to me that here I was in the Philippines and this was my chance to see something of the Ori-
ent. I wasn't in any hurry to go home, because there was
nothing in particular to go home for, so I asked Commander
Mackay if I could have a couple of days' leave to go and see
a friend of my grandmother's in Hong Kong, and insane
orders were cut for me that said I could travel 'where ver-
bally ordered.' I went to Hong Kong and then to Macao
and finally to Shanghai, which was the most exciting city
I've ever seen. I was mustered out on Staten Island.

"The Hampton years really began in 1962 with a wild summer at Francis Carpenter's Bull's Head Inn, in Bridgehamp-
ton. Pat Hemingway was there, the other, good Gardiners,
Cordelia Duke Biddle Robinson, who thought 'Mrs. Robinson' had been written for her, Pat Havens Monteagle, Car-
los and Joan Nadal, Betty Milliken, Frank Shields, Dorothy
Fields, who had a steel-trap mind, all the Gabors, Bill Blass,
and Cy Coleman, who wasn't so shy anymore. The next
year, I worked at the Mid-Ocean Bath and Tennis Club and
lived in a tiny cracker box on the dunes in Sagaponack.
Truman Capote and I passed each other on the beach.
Everyone stayed in my shack. George Frazier—dear
George, who loved clothes so—and Carol Channing and
Rona Jaffe and Julius Monk and Prince Michael of Prussia.
Carol Channing got so sunburned one weekend that we had
to take her back to New York in an ice pack to get her
swollen eyes open so she could go to work the next night.
I spent a season in East Hampton at the Hedges, and then
I went into the marvellous Irving Hotel, in Southampton. I

was there seven seasons. Formidable old ladies rocked on its veranda, and it had four enormous adjoining cottages and eleven acres of land and a beautiful garden where fashionable people got married. Bang-Bang Rutherford, who said she was going to marry me, hid a police car behind one of those giant Southampton hedges and it wasn't found for three days. I designed the room I worked in. It was called the Casino Library, and it had huge playing cards on the walls and fifteen hundred books and a fireplace and big dice cubes for tables. It was a great success. The Irving closed, and I went on for a year at the Sea Spray, two years at the Westhampton Bath and Tennis, and the summer before last I was at Zenda's, smack in the middle of Southampton. I still play winters in the islands, and occasionally I stop off for a few weeks in Palm Beach. This past summer, I went to Marbella, because I needed the change and the perspective Europe always gives me. All the Southampton people talked of committing suicide because I wouldn't be out there. A lot of my friends came over. We have pacts, little laws. One never mentions foolish or bad behavior from the night before. If you get drunk and fall down, you fall down among friends. One never talks about money. No one knows if I am rich or poor, and no one ever will. One never talks about illness. A wealthy woman I know said when a calamity occurred to a mutual acquaintance on Capri, 'We have no time on Capri for unhappiness. We are here to have fun'—which has its own undeniably wicked logic. During the day, my people have their boats and Meadow Club and cars. But I'm the night man, and from ten on they belong to me."

Absolutely Pure

Blossom Dearie

Everything about Blossom Dearie is just right. Consider her singing. She is the youngest of the four consummate supper-club singers who rule the upper regions of American song. She has a tiny voice, smaller than Mildred Bailey's or Astrud Gilberto's or Wee Bonnie Baker's; without a microphone, it would not reach the second floor of a doll house. But it is a perfect voice—light, clear, pure, resilient, and, buttressed by amplification, surprisingly commanding. Her style is equally choice, and was once described by Rogers Whitaker as going from "the meticulous to the sublime." Her diction shines (she comes from a part of eastern upstate New York noted for its accent-free speech), and she has a cool, delicate, seamless way of phrasing that is occasionally embellished by a tissue-paper vibrato. Consider her songwriting. Few first-rate singers write music, and few first-rate songwriters sing. But she has produced well over thirty tunes, and they are affecting extensions of her singing. Some, like "Hey, John," written after she appeared on a

British television show with John Lennon, are cheerful and funny ("Hey, John, look at me digging you digging me"); some, like "Home," are ruminative and gentle and pastoral; some, like "I'm Shadowing You," with lyrics by Johnny Mercer, are magic: even though one may never have heard the tune before, one immediately experiences a kind of melodic *déjà vu*. Consider her appearance and manner. She stands pole-straight, and is short and country-girl solid. Her broad face, with its small, well-spaced eyes, wide mouth, and generous, direct nose, has a figurehead strength. Her hands and feet are small and delicate. Angelic honey-blond hair falls well below her shoulders. When she is listening, she gives continuous, receptive, almost audible nods. There is no waste in her laughter, which is frequent and quick—a single, merry, high, descending triplet. And she has an almost prim manner of speaking; her sentences arrive boxed and beribboned. Consider her name. It sounds like a stage name or one of Dickens' hyperbolic inventions, but it is real. It is appropriately musical; her given name is soft and on the beat, and her surname is legato and floating. (Any other name—such as Tony Grey, which an overwrought agent once suggested—would be ludicrous.) It is also very old-fashioned; it calls to mind pinafores and lemon verbena and camomile tea. And consider her magnetism. Her old friend Jean Bach has said of her, "She is absolutely pure, and she will not compromise. She has this innocence that would take her across a battlefield unscathed. In a way, she resembles a Christian Scientist. If things go askew or don't fit in with her plans, they don't exist. She started getting under everybody's skin when she came back from Paris in the mid-fifties. I can't remember where she was working, but the place had Contact paper on the tables and out-of-work actors as waiters. It was funny when you'd take a new person to hear her. Her singing is so deceptively simple that at first there would be this 'What?' reaction, and then after a while a smile would spread across the person's face, and that would be it. You can be away from her for a long time and live your own life, and then she reappears and gets to you again. She's like a drug. She certainly has the English hooked. When she sings at Ronnie Scott's club, in London, they arrange all the chairs so that they face *her*, and there's not a sound. It's like church."

Blossom Dearie divides her year between a small Greenwich Village apartment; the family house, in East Durham, New York, where she was born; and London, whence she ventures into Scandinavia, Holland, Germany, and France. Part of her restiveness is due to economics, and part is due to an inborn need to keep on the move, to live light. Supper clubs have become almost vestigial in New York, and she is a demanding, even imperious performer who will not tolerate rude audiences. She subbed for Bobby Short at the Café Carlyle once, and, as is their wont, the swells who frequent the Café were often noisy and inattentive. Blossom Dearie repeatedly rebuked them by breaking off in midsong and announcing, in her teacup way, "You have to be a little more quiet. Some of these people are my friends and have come to hear *me!*" The swells responded by staying away, and business was poor.

She lives in a one-room apartment on the third-floor front of an old building facing Sheridan Square. On nice mornings, the room is knee-deep in sunshine. It has a *pied-à-terre* look, is furnished with a convertible sofa, a couple of yellow director's chairs, a small round sidewalk-café table, an upright piano, a tiny white desk, a record player, and several shelves of records. Blossom Dearie brewed some Irish tea, and sat down with a mug. She was wearing black pants, a white turtleneck, and a patterned black-and-off-white cardigan sweater. She laughed, crossed her legs, and rested her clasped hands on one knee. "I've decided I want to live a long time," she said. "A very long time. So I'm very conscientious about taking care of myself. I read Carlton Fredericks and Adelle Davis, and I take vitamins, especially Vitamin E, which is the wonder vitamin and helps retard the aging process. And I go to bed early and get up early. I can't stand the all-night night-club thing anymore, and any-

way what reason is there for a single person like me to stay
up late? So I've invented a new kind of show at Three,
where I am now. In fact, it's been tried at Reno Sweeney,
and maybe it'll catch on elsewhere. Since I don't feel I can
devote all my time to performing anymore, I work just four
days a week, and what I do is give an early-evening concert.
It starts at six and ends at eight. That way people can go out
and hear me and have dinner and go home to bed. No
drinks are served when I sing, but there is an intermission.
I've been cracking since six this morning. I've transposed a
new song into my key and nearly learned it, and I've practiced Billy Strayhorn's 'Lush Life,' which I've avoided for
years because it has such poor lyrics. But it is a beautiful
and quite complicated song. I've called London twice. I've
written Norman Granz, asking if he can help me get the
rights for the seven albums I made for him, so that I can re-
issue them. And I've written two of the eleven girl friends
I regularly correspond with in foreign countries. I've had a
business conference with my press agent. I'm trying to get
my life beautifully organized, and I have several projects
under way. One is starting my own place. I don't want to
buy a building or anything, just rent a room. It's going to
be *scientifically* done. I want perfect acoustics, so that people *can* talk but won't bother me. You'd be surprised what
a performer can hear—every word, every whisper. There
will be the right kind of ceiling and perfect ventilation, so
that there won't be that horrible smokiness. And the lighting will not wear my eyes out. Another project is getting
my own record label going, in addition to reissuing the
Granz things. And, finally, there are my songs, my compos-
ing, which has become very important to me. So important
that I only want to collaborate with lyricists like Johnny
Mercer. He sent me a marvellous letter not long before he
died, celebrating our friendship, and saying that since we'd
survived folk rock and soft rock and hard rock we'd go on
forever. It really pleased me."

Blossom Dearie laughed, and abruptly stood up. "I'd
make another cup of tea, but I have to tape part of the

sound track for an industrial film for a friend of mine, and the date starts in twenty minutes. The studio is on West Fifty-second Street." She walked to Sixth Avenue and got into a cab. "I have a method now when I compose," she said on the way uptown. "I write out the rhythms first, almost like a piece of drum music. Then I put the melody to that. Songs come to me in different ways. I've written quite a few of what I call tribute songs—songs for people I admire, like John Lennon and Tony Bennett. These songs are pure inspiration, pure communication between my brain and fingers and my admiration for the person, and generally they come to me quickly. Otherwise, I jot down ideas—three bars, eight bars, maybe ten—and work them out at the piano. I keep playing them over. I play them in the morning and I play them in the evening. I play them when I've had a drink and when I haven't. But I set myself a time limit. I'll work on a song for two weeks, and if it doesn't come out right I put it away for a year. But sometimes even that doesn't help, and the song never works. There's a lot of freedom now in writing songs. You don't have to follow the old thirty-two-bars-with-a-bridge pattern anymore. Songs can be any shape or length. They can be in sections or little movements. They can be a kind of string of ideas."

The recording date was in Studio B of Aura Recording, Inc. Two of the three accompanists Blossom Dearie had chosen—the reedman Hal McKusick and the bassist Jay Leonhart—were already there and noodling away on opposite sides of the room. Blossom Dearie passed out lead sheets to them and sat down at the piano, which was wedged in a far corner of the studio. Only her pants legs and the blond top of her head were visible. The recording involved her playing and singing two choruses of Harold Milan's "Going Away." She ran through the tune once with McKusick, who played the melody on flute behind her. When she had finished, she peered at him over the sheet-music rack on the piano and said, "Does that sound right?"

"Very close," McKusick replied.

"All right, let's do it again," she said, in a commander-in-chief tone. "And maybe you should improvise behind me, Hal, instead of just doing the melody."

"I think I'll switch to the alto flute this time," McKusick said. "I brought it along because I suspect it will fit very well with your sound."

After the runthrough, Blossom Dearie said she was pleased with the alto flute, which has a smoky, enfolding timbre. She got up to greet her third sideman, the drummer Al Harewood. They embraced, and she laughed and told him the date would be heavy rock and roll. The A. & R. man, Gordon Highlander, appeared, and outlined to Blossom Dearie what he wanted in the first chorus—a cheerful tempo, quiet drums, and a strong beat. As soon as Harewood was ready, they played the tune again. Blossom Dearie's unamplified voice was being drowned out by her own accompaniment, and all hands put on headphones so that they could hear her. Two takes were made, and the second was played back. Her voice was sweet and exact, and the flute set it off like the ring around a rain moon. Two more takes were made, and Highlander said they had it.

"Take five minutes," Blossom Dearie ordered. She went up to the window of the control booth and, a little girl standing in front of a toyshop, said, "Have you got any tea or Danish in there?" There was no answer, so she went around the corner and into the booth. McKusick and Leonhart started a fast, light version of Charlie Parker's "Confirmation," and Harewood joined in, dropping contented bombs on his bass drum. The date resumed, but this time thirteen takes were needed before Highlander was satisfied. It was two-thirty. Blossom Dearie took down her musicians' addresses and filled out the necessary tax and union forms. McKusick told her how fine she sounded, and thanked her for the chance to work with her. He and Leonhart left together, and Harewood, after packing up his drums and embracing her again, followed.

"Al is a terrific drummer," she said. "I've worked off and on with him for years, and he can play any kind of drums. And with so much taste." Highlander reappeared and told

Blossom Dearie that, after all, they would need some over-dubbing—just the title of the song. She looked tired but nodded. She sat on a high stool in the middle of the studio, and, putting on headphones and raising her chin, sang five "Going Away"s. Highlander asked her if she would sing them with a little more rubato. She did.

She took a cab to the Village, and said it would be nice to have some lunch. "I don't eat at night after work, but I do like a good lunch." She told the cab driver to stop at The Caffè da Alfredo, which is around the corner from the Village Vanguard. The Alfredo, which is on the parlor floor, looks out through big windows onto Seventh Avenue. It was crowded, and the only empty table was in the rear. "Oh," Blossom Dearie said. "I was hoping to sit right up front by a window, where there's lots of light and you can see everything. I hate sitting in the dark backs of places. I like light and sunshine and air." She sat down anyway, and then four people got up from a front table. "I'm going up there," she said. The table was loaded with glasses and dishes, and she asked the only waiter if she could move. He looked annoyed and shook his head. It appeared that she would sit there anyway. But all she did was let out a long "Well" and look at the menu. She ordered pea soup and a Niçoise salad.

"All I could think about up there in that studio was my mama. She passed away a little while ago. In fact, I've just come back from the country, and tonight will be the first time I've worked at Three, which is on East Seventy-second Street, in several weeks. I think they've told everyone that I've closed, so there probably won't be anyone there. My mother was in her late eighties, and she was a wonderful woman. She came over as a little girl from Oslo, where she was born. Her father was in the merchant marine, and she was raised by a grandmother. She married a rich man in New York, and they lived on West Twenty-second Street and had a house in the country—the same house she died in. It was a two-day trip in those days—up the Hudson by steamboat and twenty more miles by horse and buggy. After her husband died, she moved to the country for good. She met my father up there. When I think of my daddy—well, he was just one of those people who never seem to find their way, who never get into the niche meant for them in life. He was in the First World War, and then he was a bartender for the rest of his life. He was a lovely man. He was from Irish and Scottish parents. The name Dearie goes back in Scotland to the sixteenth century. People ask me over here if it's my real name, but everybody over there knows it. My daddy had the Irish wit—he could mimic anybody— and he was musically gifted. He could sing and dance, and he wanted to be in show business, but I guess he just didn't know how, and anyway he was not aggressive and was very much involved in his families. He had been married before, and both he and my mother had children in their earlier marriages. She had three boys, and he had one. I was their only child. It was he who named me. I was born in April, and the day I arrived a neighbor brought over some peach blossoms, and when my father saw them he said, 'That's it. We'll call her Blossom.' My mother liked Victor Herbert, but she wasn't musically inclined. She'd take me on her lap when I was two or three, and I'd pick out real tunes on the piano. I took my first piano lessons when I was five, from a Miss Parks, who lived three or four miles up the mountain. She taught me how to read. Later, I spent some time down in Washington with one of my brothers, and I studied there with a Mrs. Hill. For a year. She'd play Bach and Chopin, and if I liked it she'd tell me to learn the piece. Too many piano teachers force-feed their students. She wanted me to be a classical pianist, and thought I should study at the Peabody Conservatory, in Baltimore, when I got old enough. But I went back to the country, and I didn't study after that. I played with the high-school dance band, and I listened and listened—to Count Basie and Duke Ellington and Art Tatum. The first singer that made a real impression on me was Martha Tilton.

"After I graduated from high school, I came to New

York. I had spent a little time here before, and I'd met Dave Lambert, the singer. It was the late forties, and I lived in a midtown hotel with a bunch of girl singers. I started to sing for the first time in New York. I hung out with Dave, and we rehearsed and talked a lot about singing. And I hung out in that basement apartment Gil Evans had on West Fifty-fifth. I don't know how he ever got anything done, because there were people there twenty-four hours a day. Charlie Parker lived there for a while, and you'd generally find Dizzy Gillespie and Miles Davis and Gerry Mulligan and John Lewis. Or George Handy would be there, or George Russell or Barry Galbraith or Lee Konitz. I'd go over to Fifty-second Street, and hear Bird and Diz." She hummed the most famous version of Charlie Parker's "Embraceable You" note for note—a feat, considering that it is also one of the most subtle and difficult improvisations ever recorded. "Then I began getting jobs around New York. I was in the Show Spot, which was underneath the Byline Room, where Mabel Mercer was singing. I played piano and sang and accompanied other singers. I still like to accompany friends who sing."

The salad, which was huge, arrived, and Blossom Dearie dug in. "In 1952, when I was working at the Chantilly, I met Nicole Barclay. She and her husband owned Barclay Records, and she asked me if I'd like to work in Paris. I said yes, and took the boat. I stayed with Nicole's grandmother and studied French at Berlitz. I worked in the Mars Club in Paris, and with Annie Ross at a club in London. I formed a group called the Blue Stars of Paris; the Swingle Singers eventually grew out of it. There were four boys and four girls. The boys played instruments and sang, and the girls just sang. We had Christiane Legrand, Michel's sister, and Bob Dorough, who was in Paris accompanying Sugar Ray Robinson. We had a hit record—'Lullaby of Birdland' sung in French. There was a marvellous ambience in Paris then, an easy, hanging-out-in-cafés ambience. Bud Powell was around, and so was Don Byas. I met Norman Granz, and he recorded me there. And I met my husband, Bobby Jaspar. He was playing flute and tenor saxophone where I was working, and we became friends right away. He came from a wealthy Belgian family, and he had a degree in chemistry and spoke three languages. His father was a well-known painter. We were married in Liège, in 1955, and came back here the following year and lived in the Village. He worked with Miles Davis and J. J. Johnson. Then we separated. He had a heart condition and became ill, and he died. It was all very sad. I hope someday to get married again.

"For the next several years, I worked around New York, at the Village Vanguard, opposite Miles Davis, who became a great friend, and the original Upstairs at the Downstairs. Then I heard the album of 'Beyond the Fringe,' with Dudley Moore and Peter Cook and Jonathan Miller and Alan Bennett, and I was crazy about it. I met Dudley Moore at the Vanguard one night when he was working there, and he asked me if I was English, and I said no, but that it was a great compliment that he had thought so. We talked until five in the morning at the Vanguard, and it was through Dudley that I eventually got back to England. The English audiences seemed to take me in and like me, and I've been going every year since. In 1966, I started working for a month every summer at Ronnie Scott's club. The only thing I don't like about it is that the first show isn't until *eleven-thirty* and I don't finish until two. But I just sleep a little later in the morning to make up for it."

It was five o'clock. "Oh, my," Blossom Dearie said. "I'll just run home and get dressed and put on some makeup. I like to get to the club real early."

Three is a long, narrow brick-walled place with a bar up front, a kitchen in the middle, and a small, square room in the back. The back room has an upright piano centered on one wall and facing a dozen tables. Blossom Dearie's press agent met her in the bar and said that she had spent the day trying to get the word around that Blossom would be singing that evening. She said: "Anyway, Jean Bach, who produces Arlene Francis's radio show on WOR, is coming with a friend, and so is Harold Taylor. He used to be head of Sarah Lawrence, and he's an educational bigwig now. He's bringing Viveca Lindfors, who's dying to hear Blossom. And there may be a couple of other people." The friends arrived around six, and after Blossom Dearie had chatted with them she went into the back room and played by herself for ten minutes. Then she came out and said it was time. All nine or ten people—several had come in off the street—trooped into the back room. A heavy black curtain was drawn across the door, the lights went down, and she started in with "Ask Yourself Why," by Michel Legrand. She has a busy, luminous, childlike look when she sings. Her brow furrows from time to time, and she rocks continually from side to side. She is a swinging accompanist. Her eyes flicker back and forth between her hands and her audience. A funny song by Bob Dorough and Dave Frishberg, "I'm Hip," was followed by the Legrand–Johnny Mercer "Once Upon a Summertime." Then she did three of her own songs—"I'm Shadowing You," "Hey, John," and "I Like You, You're Nice." Before her next number, she said to the room, "What's that noise?" There was a remote humming sound. Someone said, "It's the kitchen fan. I'll see what I can do." Blossom Dearie laughed, and started "The Girl from Ipanema." She ended the first part of the concert with another funny Frishberg effort, "Peel Me a Grape."

Blossom Dearie went into the bar, and Harold Taylor bought everyone a drink. She ordered a brandy, and sat down. "Well, it took a while to get going," she said. "I'm a very gentle singer. I'm not a belter. But I try and put feeling into my songs. What I do in my way Streisand and Minnelli can't do. After I've decided how to sing a song, I sing it almost exactly the same each time, so I don't improvise while I'm singing; it's a quality I don't have. But Annie Ross has it. She can get up and sing any song in any place and knock you right out. She's so impromptu it's unbelievable. My mind wanders when I sing. I think about all sorts of things—my mama or a particular person in the audience. I think about the composer or the lyricist or one of my musicians—when I can afford to have them, that is. The words become automatic. I get nervous when I perform, but I'm told I always look perfectly calm. But then I'm a very normal person. I'm not a show-business person. I don't have the ego for that. I'm not neurotic, and I'm not crazy. I've just worked on my career. There have always been hard times financially, but perhaps all my projects will get things off the ground now. I'd sort of like to become the rage for a while."

The Human Sound

Bobby Short

Bobby Short's achievements as a performer are all the more remarkable when one considers his equipment. He has a baritone that is frequently plagued by laryngitis. He has a rapid, almost querulous vibrato, and he sometimes slides past or stops short of the note he is after. His piano playing is so unfettered it is usually accelerando—a tendency that is beautifully disguised by his accompanists, Beverly Peer (bass) and Gene Gammage (drums), who invariably keep in perfect rhythmic step. But everything in Short's style miraculously balances out. His free sense of time gives his numbers a surprised, bounding quality, his vibrato makes his phrase endings ripple like flags, his laryngitis lends his voice a searching, down sound, and his uncertain notes enhance the cheerfulness and abandon he projects. His appearance is deceptive as well. He is slight—five feet nine, with a thirty-inch waist and small, demure feet. He has an oval face, a button nose, and vaguely apprehensive eyes, all of which ride over a hedgelike mustache. But three attributes work for him. He is a faultless and inventive dresser (he is a regular on the best-dressed lists), he has a warm, princely bearing, and he has a stunning smile. The resulting impression, as one meets him, is of a tall, poised, and irresistibly attractive man.

Short lived for a long time on the eighth floor of Carnegie Hall in the apartment once occupied by Thomas Scherman, the conductor. It was the sort of place old New Yorkers covet—a small, reasonable, soundproof triplex. No sound came from outside, nor did any sound escape, so Short could sit before the baby grand in his living room at three in the morning and pound and shout with perfect propriety. The small foyer on the first floor contained a desk, a big Queen Anne armchair, a bicycle, and a staircase. A turn-around kitchen opened off it. The living room, at the top of the stairs, was two stories high, with a vaulted ceiling and a row of high windows facing north. At one end were a small bar, a bathroom, and a second set of stairs. The stairs led to a spacious balcony, which served as Short's bedroom. A bedroom window faced a small roof, where his cats, Rufus and Miss Brown, were aired. The furnishings were high-class Camp. A heavy glass-topped coffee table rested on a zebra-skin rug, and on the rug, beneath the table, were two metal lizards—one gilt, one brass. A pair of big daybeds, which were covered with bright African-looking material and leopard-skin pillows, flanked the table. Near the foyer stairs were a huge wooden lion, a stolid eighteenth-century Italian refectory table, and one of those roofed-in wicker wing chairs that still haunt old summer cottages on Naushon Island. An antler chandelier hung in the living room, and it was echoed by a Teddy Roosevelt leather chair with tusks as arms. Pictures of every description jammed the walls, and the window side of the room was lined with books and bric-a-brac.

Short occasionally models, and one afternoon he posed for a *Harper's Bazaar* sketch. He was wearing an orange-and-white cashmere turtleneck, tan slacks, and low, buckled boots, and for the drawing he had added a square-cut puma-skin coat with an otter collar, designed by Donald Brooks for Jacques Kaplan. And he had on a cowboy hat. He was leaning against a support of the balcony, his hands in the coat pockets, and he looked melancholy and distant.

The diminutive Chinese girl who was sketching him said something. "It *is* a fantastic apartment," Short said. His voice was light, melodic, yet husky. "I was away when they decided to tear down Carnegie Hall, and I guess I didn't really realize what was going on, so I didn't panic. A lot of the people who lived here did, and they moved out, and when the building was saved they had a hell of a time getting back in." He cleared his throat unavailingly. "I've had *this* bout of laryngitis for weeks. Every morning, I get on my bike and pedal over to my doctor, on the East Side. He sprays me and makes bad jokes and I pedal back, but it doesn't get any better. But then it doesn't get much of a chance. At the Café Carlyle, where I work, it's three shows a night, five nights a week. And I can't just lay off for a week or two. My responsibility is to the Carlyle. I have to be on time and I have to do everything with grace, even when I feel like saying to hell with it, when it's like pulling teeth to get myself up from my early-evening nap and shower and shave and dress and get downstairs and into a cab. The romance of being a supper-club singer! I still do private parties as well. It's extra money for Gene Gammage and Beverly Peer, and I find myself asking a lot of money. Sometimes I'm whisked down to '21' between shows to play for someone's birthday, and I've been flown to Hobe Sound and the Caribbean. And not long ago I was invited to perform at the White House. It cost me a thousand dollars, what with new clothes and transportation and all, but I was delighted I could *afford* to go. I would have been a very upset boy had I been invited and not had the money. But the Carlyle is the middle of my life. In fact, I'm hopelessly associated with it. Bobby Short of the Carlyle, despite there still being people in New York who prefer to think of me as their secret, their discovery. I started there in 1968, and in a peculiar way. George Feyer, the pianist, had been in residence for twelve years. He took off two weeks that summer, and Peter Sharp, who owns the Carlyle, asked Ahmet and Nesuhi Ertegun, of Atlantic Records, who to get as a replacement. They said, 'Get Bobby Short.' I did my best to make those two weeks as successful as anything I'd done, and when Feyer's contract ran out they offered me half a year. Feyer found a better deal elsewhere, and I work there now eight months of the year. It's physically impossible to work more than that, and anyway it doesn't make sense for me to be so available that I lose my attraction value."

He shed the fur coat and, leaning back on one of the day-beds, struck a new pose, his hands clasped behind his head and his feet on the coffee table. A tall, thin, lugubrious-looking man in blue denim work clothes came in.

"How was your weekend, Wendell?" Short asked him.

"I'm not feeling so well. A cold."

"Are you congested? Well, I've got just the pill for you. Take one now and one tonight." Wendell went upstairs, put leashes on the cats, and took them out on the roof. Wendell cleans and cooks and does odd jobs for Short three days a week.

"I think the Carlyle is probably one of the last places in the world where you can drink tea with your pinkie comfortably out. It attracts royalty. It's not unusual to have a baroness or a princess around, as well as Mrs. Palm Beach Gardner, Mrs. Winston Frost, and Bunny Mellon. My dressing room, which is on the fourth floor, above the Café Carlyle, is really one of the maids' rooms that the hotel provides for the servants such people generally travel with. But you can come into the Carlyle wearing practically anything. It is big enough and elegant enough and grand enough not to be affected by unusual attire among its patrons. I'd been to the hotel several times before I worked there, and I was always treated beautifully. I must deal with the people who come solely to see Bobby Short. They make all sorts of complaints, written and verbal. 'Mr. Short didn't sing at all during his first show last night,' or 'Mr. Short finished his second set ten minutes early.' My God! And if I sing too many Negro songs, the Negro patrons get self-conscious and the whites think I'm being militant. Imagine Bessie Smith's 'Gimme a Pigfoot' being considered militant! Everyone who sings in a café has to have something about him that says, 'Come close but not too close.' But people often get too close, too pully on you. Beverly and Gene and I have been together for a long while, and we have accumulated a lot of friends. But we must think of ourselves as caterers at a party. After all, the waiters and bartenders can't get drunk, and I can't sit down with friends between shows and have a quart of champagne or six whiskeys. It takes some stuff to remember your place so long as you're earning a living, and I'll always have to earn a living. If I get overly friendly, the audience thinks, 'Oh, it doesn't matter. We know him so well that we don't have to listen!'

"The people who come to hear me are a mixed bag, and they range in age from eighteen to seventy-five. A lot of them are rich, but I have lived among the wealthy and bizarre so long that their ways don't bother me. I also get professional football players, and Leontyne Price, who is a great friend. Alice Faye and Bart Howard come in, and Craig Claiborne was there a while ago with a lady from Texas who's a billionairess. The clergy come in, and so do neighborhood ladies, who can walk safely home together. The whole clutch from Elaine's comes in, including Jack Richardson and Norman Mailer. Norman even wrote a poem about me once. But musicians come into the Carlyle, too—people like Miles Davis and Cy Coleman and Joe Williams and Marian McPartland. And a lot of fashion people, but they have followed me all my career—the designers and the models, the manufacturers. Senator Javits and his wife are regulars, and there are a lot of French people, and I speak French to them, of course. And there have been a good many young people, including rock groups. They give one hope. People say that graciousness is finished, but it isn't. My people respect graciousness. They are ready to be gracious and they respond to graciousness."

The girl finished her sketches. She and Short packed the fur coat in a box, and she staggered out with it under one arm and her drawings under the other. Wendell shouted up the stairs that a bottle of champagne had exploded in the freezer. Short slapped his forehead. "Oh dear! That's terrible. That's the worst thing I've *ever* done. I put that in there last night before some friends came, but they drank something else and I forgot about it. Is it bad, Wendell?"

"Yes, it's in little pieces. After I clean up, do you want me to go out and get a roast or something?"

"All right, and some Boston lettuce and orange juice."

Short went over to the bar and poured a ginger ale. "I only eat once a day, at lunch," he said. "I can't eat before I work. If I do, I can't breathe when I sing, or else all the wine and cheese come up. Sometimes I go somewhere fancy for lunch—that's my treat for the day—or I cook something here. When I'm not working, I can put together a decent bœuf bourguignon for six or eight people. After they leave, I strip off all my clothes and go down to the kitchen and wash up. It takes me a couple of hours, but it's the best therapy in the world."

A radio, which had been playing, began a Duke Ellington tune.

"I got to know the Ellington band-pack in the early forties," Short said, "when I was living in Los Angeles and was more or less adopted by Harold Brown, a pianist and the brother of Lawrence Brown, Ellington's trombonist. The band would come to the Coast—and those parties! They went on until eight or nine in the morning. All the liquor you could drink and all the available girls in town and Art Tatum playing the piano in a corner. I've been unswerving since then—a lifelong devotee. Some of those things Duke wrote in the last thirties and early forties— they're mind-bending. The last time I saw the band they were at the Rainbow Grill, that great glassed-in place up above the city. It was a total New York night. My date was an English girl, a fan of mine, and the Duke had a thing going. Everybody was there. Tony Bennett. Sylvia Syms.

They both sang. Then someone saw me. I told them to go away and shut up, but Duke got me up there, and I chose 'Rose of the Rio Grande,' simply because I wanted to hear Lawrence Brown's great solo on it. He played it, and I found out later that Duke and Lawrence had had words earlier that night, and Lawrence had told him, 'No solos tonight.' It was a great compliment."

Short looked at his watch. "I have to go down to the photography department at Macy's to get an old picture of my mother restored." He picked up a dark oval photograph, torn and faded, of a pretty woman with long hair and deep, faintly smiling eyes. "It will be in my book, *Black and White Baby*, which I just finished the transcript of the other night, at two-thirty in the morning. It's about the first seventeen years of my life—my life as a show-biz kid. My mother is remarkable. She lives with my oldest sister, Naomi, in Danville, Illinois, where I was born. Mother was tiny, never weighing more than a hundred and fifteen pounds, and, as you can see, very pretty. When I was a kid, she worked all day, and when she wasn't at her job she was at church or in a P.T.A. meeting or trying to keep her house in order. She was a domestic, as most of her friends were, and she worked from seven-thirty in the morning until early evening. She was ambivalent. Her pride drove her out to work all day, using every avenue of strength she had, but then when I was ten she'd let me go and play the piano and sing in the local roadhouses—provided she knew the mother of someone in the band. She let me do this when she wouldn't allow a jazz record or a blues record in the house and when she thought it unthinkable to go into show business, which was considered a one-way road straight to Hell, thanks to the Puritanical nonsense the Negroes borrowed from the whites. But it was the Depression and things were very rough, and I know that the three or four dollars I brought home on Saturday nights were used to pay the gas bill or buy clothes and books for us children. Mother never cracked more than ten dollars a week as a domestic, and here I could make almost half that in one night's work. I think she respected me for it.

"I was born the ninth of ten children. There were never more than seven of us alive at once. My mother and father came from Kentucky, but they met in Danville. It's about a hundred and twenty-five miles south of Chicago, and it hovers close to the Indiana line. It was the best of all possible places to be poor in the Depression—in a small town where there were no racial pressures. There was a small colored population and an old colored section, but the town was at least superficially integrated. We lived in a newer section, where there were whites. Very often I was the only Negro in my class. I never knew Father terribly well. He was slender and had a marvellous mustache, which was balanced by a tonsure that I inherited. He went through eight years of school, and then his father sent him to four more at Frankfort College, which was more like a high school then. His father was not wealthy, but he owned farms here and there. He'd been born at the end of slavery, but he was a freedman. My father had a talent for mathematics, and he was brilliant at speedwriting. He had gifts that could have made him a much greater man than he was. He held a number of white-collar jobs, civil-service jobs. He ran for justice of the peace in Danville, and he won. But he liked the coal mines. When the Depression hit, he went back to Kentucky to the mines. He sent us money and came to see us twice a year. But the mines were his Waterloo. I was about nine or ten when he died."

Miss Brown shot down the stairs from the bedroom, leaped up on the pillows on the daybed, and lay there, watching Rufus, who was creeping along the base of the bookcase. "Rufus!" Short shouted. "Stop it!" Rufus slid across the floor on his belly, his eyes on Miss Brown. "Go on! Enough! Scat!" Rufus catapulted up the stairs and disappeared under the bed. Short picked up a handful of pistachio nuts from a bowl and began to open them.

"There was a piano in our house, as there was in every

house then, and I taught myself to play and sing. I listened to Ivie Anderson and to Bing Crosby, and once in a while I'd get a good hot radio program from Chicago, and bands like Fess Williams' and Walter Barnes' came through town. I left Danville for the first time when I was eleven and a half. A couple of booking agents came through and heard me sing and play, and they took me off to Chicago—with my mother's permission, of course. I lived on the West Side with a Catholic family from New Orleans, which appealed to my mother, and I went to a Catholic school. When I left Danville, I had no idea what image I projected. There I was, a child sitting in tails at the piano and singing 'Sophisticated Lady' and 'In My Solitude' in a high, squeaky voice in astonishing keys. The lyrics meant nothing to me, and they must have sounded strange to other people coming out of a child's mouth. So I changed and sang things like 'Shoe Shine Boy' and 'It's a Sin To Tell a Lie.' But I could not find it within me to believe that I *was* a child. And I didn't like being a child, because I couldn't stand the patronization connected with childhood. Moreover, it was never in me to be the best colored singer or the best colored student. I simply wanted to be the best singer and the best student. But I have a respect for my race that might surprise some of the people who discovered just six months ago that they are black. I was brought up in such a way that doesn't allow any head-hanging. There is nothing about me that can be called non-white, but I consider myself fortunate because I'm not so well known that people accept me only for my fame. A long time ago, I discovered that the best advertisement for a minority is that member who, without being Uncle Tom, takes the time to mesh with whatever exists socially. He makes it that much easier for the next member who comes along.

"That winter, I worked mostly around Chicago. I did some broadcasting over N.B.C., and a lot of so-called 'club' dates at places like the Sheraton Hotel. I'd be part of one-night shows that included an orchestra, tap-dancers, and other singers. I became the colored counterpart of Bobby

Breen. I got thirty or thirty-five dollars for each club date, but of course I had to buy clothes and pay tuition and give something to the family I lived with. When I finished school, in June of 1937, I was twelve and a half. But I didn't go home. I went East. New York wasn't easy, because I started there from scratch, performing all times of day and night for bookers. But I worked at the Frolic Café, over the Winter Garden Theatre, at La Grande Pomme, and at the Apollo, in Harlem. The audiences at the Apollo were used to Pigmeat Markham and Butter Beans and Susie and Moms Mabley, and I was obviously a downtown act. They didn't care about my white tie and tails. All they wanted was to be turned on. They probably all had kids my age at home who danced and sang anyway.

"The New York thing came to an abrupt end early in 1938. I suddenly realized that there I was—a kid with two years of show biz and all the mannerisms of an adult—and I didn't like it, so I went back to Danville and stayed there four years, until I finished high school. It was a funny adjustment to make at first. I had come off what was regarded as the big time. My mother said I couldn't work for tacky people in tacky places after working in grand hotels and grand theatres for grand people. So I didn't work for the first year, but I began to feel the economic pressures and I went back to work in earnest. I had more pizzazz by then, and I was a professional. I sought out the best hotels and taprooms around Danville, and after a while I became solvent and could dress myself properly and even indulge myself. I finished high school in 1942, and a month later I opened at the Capitol Lounge, in Chicago. The rage was boogie-woogie. I thought it was cheap. I made up my mind there was something better. I had heard Hildegarde on records, and of course she was the queen then. She had the slickest night-club act of all time. It was produced down to the last sigh. Even down to a blue spotlight that brought out the color in the red roses that invariably stood by her piano. She would record whole Broadway scores, and she sang Vernon Duke and Cole Porter and the Gershwins and

Noël Coward, and through her I became aware of the Broadway kind of score, of the mystique of the Broadway musical.

"In 1943, I went to the Beachcomber, in Omaha, where I worked for a week opposite Jimmy Noone, the New Orleans clarinettist, and for a week opposite Nat Cole. Nat and I became friends and remained friends until he died. He was a sly, funny man, and he'd sit in the back room and watch me—a smart-aleck nineteen-year-old—performing out front, and he'd laugh and say, when I came off, 'What are you *doing* to these people?' I got a job in Los Angeles with Mike Reilly—'The Music Goes Around and Around and It Comes Out Here' Reilly—in the Radio Room. He had a comedy band, and they threw flounders at the audience, and that sort of thing. I first heard there about Mabel Mercer and Cy Walter, and I became deeply immersed in Rodgers and Hart. And Don McCrae, who is really Don Redman and who wrote 'Practice Makes Perfect,' came to my house with a huge stack of out-of-the-way songs and told me to learn them. My job at the Radio Room ended a couple of months later. Another comedy band had come in, and the act involved smoke pouring out of the top hat the leader wore. The smoke was flour, and it spewed out all over me, and I was in black tie. After the first show, I refused to go back on, and I was dismissed. I worked around, mostly at private parties for fifty dollars a night, and at the old Trocadero Ballroom, filling in for Dorothy Donegan. Then I got a gig in Milwaukee, where I appeared opposite the Art Tatum trio, with Tiny Grimes on guitar and Slam Stewart on bass. Tatum will always be my idol, and it was marvellous to get to know him. He had the same sort of sly humor that Nat Cole had. He enjoyed pretty ladies and he drank a *lot* of beer. There was no condescension, and in a strange way I think he even admired me, even though he never talked about music. But it always astonished me that for the most part the people who came to hear him didn't really know what they were hearing."

Short jumped up. "Macy's awaits me." He reappeared

ten minutes later. He was wearing a sensationally well-tailored Glen-plaid suit. His shoes were dark, his shirt was a pale blue, and his modestly wide tie was navy with white polka dots. He got a cab on Seventh Avenue. He conducted his business at Macy's in a sparkling way, as if *he* were waiting on the saleslady. In the cab, he had said that he had gone from Milwaukee to the Chase Hotel, in St. Louis, where Hildegarde was the main attraction. It was the first time he had seen her work. Her manager heard him and called Herbert Jacoby, who, along with Max Gordon, owned the Blue Angel, in New York. Jacoby went out to St. Louis and asked Short to come to the Blue Angel the following spring. "Eddie Mayehoff was on the bill," Short said on the escalator. "And Irene Bordoni and Mildred Bailey, and of course I was just the opener. For a long time, I thought my engagement at the Blue Angel was not successful, but I learned later that Jacoby and Gordon often cancelled new acts after the first night. I stayed for a full four weeks. I shared a dressing room with Mildred Bailey, and I got some interesting insights into her. Despite that enormous *poitrine* and her barrel shape and those toothpick legs, she was very vain. She had a lovely face and beautiful skin, and she'd sit at her dressing table in front of the mirror the whole time between shows, fixing her face and staring at herself. We talked constantly, but she never once took her eyes off herself and looked at me."

Short walked from Macy's to Brooks Brothers, where he wanted to look at some dress shirts and pumps. "I met Mabel Mercer, too, for the first time, and Bart Howard, who gave me a lot of his songs. I longed to belong to Mabel's intimate circle, and I knew I had to come back to New York one day on a more permanent basis. Mabel has worked as viciously hard as I have. She has always sung in small places without microphones, and she thinks microphones are abominable. Mabel is much more fragile than I. She is, as we know it in America, the outstanding personage of our kind of art. When I first met her, the thing that struck me was her repertoire. I was involved in the same pursuit, and it was true serendipity. Even when she sang a song I knew, it came to be totally fresh. I can't think of any singer who is true to himself who has avoided being influenced by Mabel Mercer. People have accused me of stealing from other performers, but that's nonsense. What one does is absorb the *feeling* generated by a great *singer* like Mabel. She is an enormously private person, and I'm flattered that we have a friendship.

"After the Blue Angel, I went back to California and worked off and on on Monday nights for three or four months at the Haig, a kind of a shack on Wilshire Boulevard, across from the Ambassador Hotel. It was run by a show-biz nut named Johnny Bernstein, and he kept bringing me obscure show tunes. Between him and Don McCrae, my repertoire became sizable. The periods in between my stints at the Haig were very poor. I lived with Harold Brown and his wife. They fed me and slept me and even gave me pocket money, or I wouldn't be here today. Then I got a job at the Café Gala. It was in a big house on Sunset Boulevard which had been bought by the Baroness d'Erlanger for Johnny Walsh to sing in. He was a tall, fantastically handsome Irishman with white hair and beautifully tailored clothes, and he had the largest repertoire I'd ever heard. The Gala was the most chic club in California, or the West, for that matter. It was always filled with ex-New Yorkers, and you'd see Lena Horne and Lennie Hayton and Monty Woolley and Cole Porter. Walsh sold the Gala to a man named Jim Dolan. He gave me a one-week contract, but I stayed from July of 1948 to the fall of 1951. I became the mainstay, announcing shows and playing interim piano. Felicia Sanders worked there, and Bobby Troup and Dorothy Dandridge and Stella Brooks and Sheila Barrett. Eventually, a neon sign appeared on the roof: 'Jim Dolan Presents Bobby Short.' I acquired a new apartment and met all sorts of people high up in the movie business, and international people. I fell into a velvet-lined rut. In fact, one night Olga San Juan turned to Leonard Spigelgass at the Gala and said, 'Who this is Bobby Short? Why isn't he in films, why isn't he making a lot of records?' Spigelgass replied, 'He's too chic.' And that was the truth. I had become the young colored boy who was all chic and who dined at the Café Jay, which sat just twenty, fifteen of them invariably the biggest Hollywood stars, and that was as far as I could go. People kept telling me, 'Go to New York, Bobby. Get out of here and go to New York.' I knew I wasn't ready for New York, but I did go to Paris, first class, by plane."

At Brooks, Short tried on some pumps. "That lady sitting over there is Erika Lund," he said, "and she worked at the Gala when I was there. I still sing one of her songs." They greeted each other warmly, and he told her to stop by the Café Carlyle. Old Home Week continued at the shirt counter, where the dapper, middle-aged salesman told Short he had once been with Young & Rubicam and that he used to go to the Beverly Club, at Lexington and Fiftieth, to hear him. Short looked pleased, bought six shirts, and told *him* to stop by the Carlyle.

Short went over to the Algonquin and ordered a beer. "I just love this place," he said. "It's an oasis in this mad city. Well, the rest of that year in Paris was insane. I worked for Spivy and I worked at the Embassy Club, in London, several times. I had an atelier in the most fashionable *arrondissement* in Paris. I had a maid, a private French tutor, I ate well, and when I was in London I bought all the clothes I could. Then it was back to L.A. and the Gala, and in the beginning of 1954 I met Phil Moore, the arranger and composer, and he became my manager. He figured out how my act could be enlarged, controlled, polished. The first thing he did was to put me in a room in Los Angeles with Larry Bunker, the drummer, and Rollie Bundock, the bassist. We made a tape and Phil sold it to Nesuhi and Ahmet Ertegun. Then I was flown to New York by Dorothy Kilgallen, as a birthday present for her husband, Dick Kollmar. The record came out, Dorothy paved the way in her column, and I got the job at the Beverly Club. I went on to the Red Carpet, Le Cupidon, and back to the Blue Angel, where I had top billing and made a thousand dollars a week. I worked the Living Room, the Weylin Hotel, and the Arpeggio. During the summers, I went back to California for short stints, and to Florida, for the first time, and Chicago. Early in the sixties, after I'd been here at the Sheraton-East, the old Ambassador Hotel, Herbert Jacoby and a rich friend and myself took over a room on East Fifty-fourth Street and called it Le Caprice. Herbert had always coveted an *haute-cuisine* French restaurant, which Caprice was, and my trying to cater to an eating clientele instead of a drinking one didn't make it. We lasted a year and three months. Then came the heavy time for Mr. Short. I hadn't taken any salary at all for the last three months at the Caprice, and I had gone through all my savings. I was on my uppers. During the summer of 1965, I didn't work in New York at all, except for occasional weekends, and I ended up in Provincetown and Cleveland. But that winter I was lucky enough to have a standup part in the 'New Cole Porter Revue,' down at Square East, in the Village. A while after that, I got a job in the upstairs room at L'Intrigue, over on West Fifty-sixth Street. I handled my own lights, I seated guests. It fed my cats, paid the rent, and kept me alive. For the next few years, I subsisted in Boston at Paul's Mall, at the Living Room here, and at places like the Playboy Club in London. The night-club business was not what it had been."

The Café Carlyle is a small, oblong room (it seats under two hundred) on one side of the Madison Avenue entrance of the Hotel Carlyle. A tiny sit-down bar is concealed behind pillars, and against the opposite wall, on a low dais, is a grand piano. There are banquettes around the other walls, which are covered by murals, and the center of the room is taken up by a dozen tables. It is a dark, dowdy, comfortable place. Short appeared at nine-thirty, resplendent in a dinner jacket and pleated white shirt, and sat down in semidarkness at the piano, flanked on one side by Gene Gammage and on the other by Beverly Peer. No lights went on; he simply started to play. He looked solemn and detached and private, as if he were playing for himself late at night in his living room. It was a graceful, flowing display. He did a Gershwin medley, "Perdido," the theme from "Exodus," a blues, and several other tunes. His style bears a loose, enthusiastic resemblance to Art Tatum's—it is florid and arpeggioed and slurred—and by the time he had played ten or so tunes a considerable head of steam had been built up. The lights went on, and he began to sing Cole Porter's "Let's Fly Away." It was immediately clear that it would be a difficult night. His laryngitis was compounded by a faulty microphone, and the crowd was noisy. During his third song, he stopped abruptly when new arrivals began loudly *"Comment-ça-va"*ing the people at the next table. Looking over their heads with a slight smile, his hands resting on the raised keyboard cover, he waited until the room subsided, and then began where he had left off.

After the last number, he greeted several people, then sat down at a table. He mopped his face and ordered a glass of ice water and hot tea with honey. The headwaiter apologized for the microphone; the repairman had promised to come but had not. Short smiled and croaked, "I know. I know. Phil Moore told me that it really doesn't matter what a performer does. It's a question of how many dishes the busboys drop and of whether or not the microphones work. And it's up to the audience, too. When you get a bad one, you work harder and harder and sing louder and louder to compensate, and *they* talk louder and louder to compensate for you. But a bad microphone is like playing with a drunken drummer. If I were on a stage, removed, it would be different, but I'm practically within touching distance of everyone here. On top of that, I know most of them. Those are Shaker Heights people over there, and the group that came in and made all the noise includes Liza Minelli's estranged husband, and back against the wall is Geraldine Stutz, of Bendel, and her husband. Of course, one night you come in and the piano is in tune, the boys feel wonderful, I feel wonderful, and the audience is rotten. Another night, I feel perfectly rotten and the audience sits there as though they were in church. You must never be angry or uptight in the gut; you have to be free and loose. Singing itself is such pure expression. The human sound is the most touching in the world; it's exemplified by someone like Ray Charles. He has that kind of getting inside a song and finding something that the composer himself didn't know was there. And a good performer can't be carrying on emotionally when he sings. You simply can't sing well with a lump in your throat. Take 'I Still Believe in You.' It has one of my favorite lyrics of all time. It's by Rodgers and Hart, and was dropped from a 1930 show called '*Simple Simon*' before the show opened. I first heard Charlotte Rae sing it, and I've known it for a year, but for a long time I could not bring myself to sing it without breaking up. Finally, I absorbed the song, and now I can do it."

Geraldine Stutz went by, and Short stood up and spoke to her, then poured more honey in his tea.

"I guess I have several hundred songs in my repertoire, and when I'm requested to sing a song I've never sung in my life I find that I suddenly know all the words, and we figure out a key and we're off. I can sing songs I haven't sung in ten years, and the only ones I ever have to brush up on are things I sang as a child. Actually, I wish I *could* push some of the lyrics I've got in my head out and replace them with newer material, but that's an occupational hazard; you become a kind of singing Smithsonian. I'm interested in all kinds of *good* songs. Sometimes the lyrics grab me, sometimes the song itself. It's not often that the marriage is perfect. But the Gershwins can be counted on, and Cole Porter made both ends work. Rodgers and Hart were brilliant. Vernon Duke wasn't always fortunate enough to find good lyricists. Yip Harburg was good with him, and so was Ira Gershwin. But I don't think Vernon was easy to work with. I love Harold Arlen and Johnny Mercer, and when they collaborated on the score of 'St. Louis Woman' it was almost too much of a good thing. Johnny Mercer displayed a homespun façade in his work, but he was capable of turning out a truly sensational lyric. I worship Fats Waller, but I feel inadequate with his material. But I do all the Ellington and Strayhorn I can pick up. I get into Noël Coward and Ivor Novello, among the English songwriters. My thinking English friends bring them over to me. I prefer Coward to Novello; his songs hold up beautifully. I feel almost intellectual when I sing one. It's just like reading a Huxley novel. I like some of the things that Charles Trenet and Jean Sablon sang in the thirties and forties in France. English songs tend to be sentimental, but French songs are unique—tough, and the thirty-two-bar form be damned. But it is the Americans who excel at writing popular songs. You can go anywhere in the world and hear American songs."

For his second show, he sang a dozen songs, among them a fascinating, meditative "I Can't Get Started." Then came a couple of Burt Bacharach songs, a swinging "Nashville Nightingale," a slow Stella Brooks blues, the Bessie Smith "Cake Walkin' Babies," and a long, intense reading of "Bye Bye Blackbird." In the fast numbers, his tempos raced in all directions, his face took on a strained, almost diabolical look, he reared back and shouted, and he often ended a song by flinging his right hand out, leaping to his feet, and standing statue-still, his eyes fixed high on the back wall of the room. For slow ballads, the lights were lowered and he sang quietly, his voice husky and small, his accompaniment full of soft tremolos and runs. The audience came around quickly, and by the time he had finished "Blackbird" there wasn't a murmur in the room.

He sat down and ordered more tea with honey, and talked about the songs he'd just sung, a couple of which were unfamiliar. " 'You Better Love Me' is from *High Spirits*, which was based on *Blithe Spirit*, and 'Sand in My Shoes' is from *Kiss the Boys Goodbye*, the 1940 Loesser–Schertzinger thing. It was never a terribly successful song, but it's the most requested thing I do. That 'Can't Get Started' I love. Ira Gershwin wrote lots of stanzas, and he's a nifty one for going back and rewriting his lyrics years later. Did I do 'By Strauss'? That was from a 1936 revue, and it was by the Gershwins. Bert Lahr and Beatrice Lillie were in it, and Vernon Duke wrote his 'Now' for it. It was, I believe, first recorded by George Byron, the tenor who married Eva Kern, Jerome's widow. It was on the General label, and Byron's pianist on the date was Bobby Tucker. A voice coach who took a shine to me in Hollywood in the early forties introduced it to me. Then I did a couple of Bacharachs. 'Nashville Nightingale' was a Gershwin number, written in the late twenties. Vernon Duke gave me it, too. He never pushed any of his own songs, but he would sit with me for hours and push everybody else's. He came to New York once with fourteen unknown Gershwin tunes and wanted me to record them immediately, but unfortunately nothing came of it. 'It Never Entered My Mind' was from *Higher and Higher*, a 1940 Rodgers and Hart effort, and I think I first heard Shirley Ross sing it on an old Blue Seal Decca. The 'Bye Bye Blackbird' is a little different, because I interpolate part of 'I'm a Little Blackbird Looking for a Bluebird.' "

Short looked up. The room was packed, and the lobby outside the glass entrance door was filled with people waiting for tables. He smiled. "I better get up to my maid's room and change again."

A Queenly Aura

Mabel Mercer

Alec Wilder, a brilliant and iconoclastic composer, who is quick to damn and slow to praise, recently set down his thoughts about Mabel Mercer: "She transmutes popular song to the extent that by means of her taste, phrasing, and intensity it becomes an integral part of legitimate music. When she sings a song, it is instantly ageless. It might have been composed the day before, but, once given the musical dignity of her interpretation, it is no longer a swatch of this season's fashion but a permanent part of vocal literature. She has never made the slightest attempt to sing in the manner one expects of popular singers. As a result, those who assume that a 'swinging' style is a prerequisite of a singer of such songs are sometimes thrown off or baffled by her constant dignification (if I may risk such a word) of otherwise casual songs. It is not that she is unaware of the rhythmic looseness of an up-tempo song or of a slow blues. It is rather that her purpose is to present a musical point of view which has more to do with the intimate concert hall than with a casual night spot. That impalpable quality known as showmanship is, in her case, inapplicable. Rather [she exhibits] graciousness, magnetism, profound calm, and, most of all, complete authority."

More by accident than by design, Mabel Mercer has spent most of her career singing in supper clubs, and so she is, in the best sense, a miniaturist, who sings to small audiences in small rooms about seemingly small things—a remembered spring, a broken romance, a new lover, a lost childhood. But the supper club—that royal relative of the night club—has almost been obliterated by television, and its patrons have dwindled and grown old. Few of the sort of special, witty, poetic songs Mabel Mercer sings are written anymore, partly because they would seem hopelessly archaic and mannered and partly because the insouciant musical theatre that bred so many of them no longer exists. Moreover, of all performing artists, singers grow old most quickly, and within the past decade Mabel Mercer's voice has shrunk, and it has become difficult for her to sustain a note with any effect. Instead, she has perfected what Wilder calls a "graceful parlando"—a way of melodiously talking her songs. Her phrasing and choice of tones and insuperable diction—her style, in short—remain not only intact but inspired; it is simply that rests have supplanted the flow of melody between tones. Her singing in her prime was unique. It lay somewhere between the concert hall and jazz. She had a rich, low mezzo-soprano and a considerable range, and her best tones had the elastic, power-in-reserve sound of formal singers. Her phrasing was jazzlike in that she often placed her notes in surprising places and often used jazz timbres. She was able, in an uncanny way, to make her voice encompass not only many moods but their attendant colors—the purples of love, the blues of sorrow, the yellows of humor and good cheer, the black of despondency. She was a superb dramatic singer who could handle with equal ease the *Sturm und Drang* of Kurt Weill's "Trouble Man" and the bittersweet feeling of Wilder's "Did You Ever Cross Over to Sneden's?" Every song she sang seemed to

be fashioned out of the fabric of her own experience, and to
be an individual offering to each one of her listeners. And
she still is a marvellous comic singer, who, by surrounding
the right word with silence or by dipping it in a growl, invariably provokes laughter. Above all was her easy, alabas-
ter technique—the ingenious phrasing, the almost elocution-
ary diction, the dynamics (she never shouted and she never
relied on the staginess of the near-whisper), the graceful
melodic push, the quick rhythmic sense, and, always, the
utter authority.

Mabel Mercer was, and is, just as irresistible visually. Seeing her is not a fleeting experience; it recalls the brief, stunning sequence on television during the mid-fifties in which
Queen Elizabeth, in New York, was passing in review of
some worthy body. The cameras, on closeup, studied her
face as she stopped and spoke to people. She looked drawn
and tired, but she was unfailingly gracious and gentle. It
was an unforgettably attractive human display. Mabel Mercer has precisely that queenly aura. Indeed, she is now of
Victorian proportions—short, quite round, and with fine,
luminous eyes and a shy child's smile. Her ramrod posture,
swan neck, and high cheekbones make her seem taller than
she is. And so do her high forehead, which supports a cloud
of dark, short hair, and the long, sumptuous, often low-
necked gowns she wears. She sings seated in a throne-like
armchair, and she invariably wears a bright silk shawl tossed
loosely over her shoulders. She is a study in composure.
Her chin slightly lifted, her body pitched slightly forward,
she keeps her torso motionless and her hands clasped in her
lap except when, several times during a song, she describes
a series of illustrative arabesques in the air with her right
hand or holds it out palm up, as if she sensed a shower. She
sings with her eyes half closed, and she moves her head only
to emphasize a phrase or word. (She has not used a microphone until recent years, but, placed casually to one side of
her chair, it is unobtrusive.) At the close of each set, she
gets up quickly and ducks out of the room. In a minute or
two, she resumes her chair and sings two or three encores

(she will sometimes sing upward of thirty songs in a sitting), and she is done. Her audiences, released, tend to surface slowly; she recalls times when she has finished singing and there has been no applause at all—presumably because of a surfeit of emotion among her listeners.

When Mabel Mercer came to New York, the city was garlanded with supper clubs, and she worked without pause for twenty years. The fervency of her following was such that between 1941 and 1957 she sang in only two clubs—Tony's and the Byline Room—and when the Byline burned down a new one was immediately built for her. But work has not been plentiful of late. She has appeared at the Café Carlyle and Downstairs at the Upstairs, and she has given several S.R.O. concerts with Bobby Short. Twilights, though, are often the capstone of the day, and for a couple of seasons Mabel Mercer held forth brilliantly at the St. Regis Room. She lived in the St. Regis during her engagements, and when, during one of them, a reporter from a midwestern paper called to find out if he could visit her there, he was told, a few days later, that she was dubious. She wondered what they would talk about, and she said that there really wasn't much to her life; she had been in show business since she was fourteen, and that was it. Mabel Mercer pursues privacy, she treasures it, she embraces it. Despite constant requests, she refuses to write an autobiography. But after she had conferred with Harry Beard, her manager and amanuensis, she set a day for the meeting. The reporter arrived at the hotel and called her room, but there was no answer, and there was no message at the desk. He turned around, and a short, stocky figure in a brown tweed coat and a long woollen scarf was emerging from the elevator.

"Oh, my," she said, putting a hand up to her mouth. Her voice was low and her accent elegant. "I forgot all about you. I have to go out and pick up a couple of gowns for the Dick Cavett show, which I'm supposed to tape tomorrow. I've done very few TV talk shows, and I'm rather nervous about it."

The reporter asked if he could go with her.

"Oh, certainly not," she said. "But come to the Cavett show with me. They're sending a limousine at one. Harry Beard will be with us, and Jimmy Lyon, my accompanist. But while you're here, come and look at the room." She moved slowly through the lobby, rocking slightly from side to side and threading her way between small mountains of luggage. She stopped just short of the King Cole Bar, at a pair of open glass doors. The St. Regis Room seated perhaps seventy-five, and it was posh. The floor was carpeted, the ceiling was blue, and there were love seats and leather chairs and small tables. Mirrors and gold paper covered the walls. To the right of the doors was a tiny, almond-shaped stand, with a grand piano, a microphone, and a French Provincial armchair. The room was full of lunching women.

"It's nice, isn't it?" she asked. She opened her coat and put her hands on her hips. "I do two shows on Tuesdays, Wednesdays, and Thursdays, and three on Fridays and Saturdays. Then I have my two days off, so that I can get up to my house in Chatham, New York, and have a nice rest. They wanted me to start my first show at nine or nine-thirty, and I told them that was too early. Much too early for my people. So I start around ten, and then what did they do at first but close the doors of the room at ten sharp and keep the people waiting outside until the second show began! 'Here, what's this?' I told them. 'You can't do that. These people rush away from their coffee to get here on time and find the doors shut in their faces.' So we've changed all that. They still close the doors, but they bring the late-comers in by a back way. Well, I must go. I'm sorry about today, but you be here at one sharp tomorrow."

The reporter was, and a few minutes later Mabel Mercer came out of the elevator. She was greeted by a tall, stooped man with short gray hair and thick glasses. He was Harry Beard. She was carrying a clothesbag over one arm, and she handed it to Beard. "I've brought two gowns, one black and one white."

"They'll tell you which one they want you to wear, Ma-

bel," he said. "They have their own ideas about these things."
He spoke in a concerned, measured way, a nanny clucking
over a charge.

A young, good-looking priest rushed up, expectantly
smiling.

"Oh, Peter. It's you. How nice," Mabel Mercer said. Peter O'Brien, a Jesuit, spends most of his waking hours shep-
herding the jazz pianist Mary Lou Williams. He and Mabel
Mercer embraced.

"I just stopped by to give you a cheer and see how you
were," he said. "I've been moved to another church, at
Eighty-third and Park, but I'll still have plenty of time to
be with Mary."

"Park Avenue," Beard said. "Well, Peter, you've moved
that much closer to Heaven."

O'Brien laughed, and said he'd stop by one evening next
week. A short, thin gray-haired man in a black raincoat and
a dinner jacket appeared—Jimmy Lyon.

"I'll go and see where the limousine is," Beard said.

"The Cavett people changed the time of the taping from
six in the evening to now," Mabel Mercer said. "I told them
it's practically impossible for a singer to sing so early. I
don't get upstairs from the St. Regis Room until almost
three, and I can't just pop out of bed and start performing."

Beard reappeared with the driver. "I put the gowns in
the trunk," he said. Everyone got into the car and headed
for Cavett's studio, which is on Fifty-eighth, between Seventh and Broadway.

"I can't very well practice in my room at the hotel,
either," Mabel Mercer said. "The neighbors would say,
'What's that crazy woman doing singing in her room?' I
did get a reaction like that once in the country, when I was
learning a new song. I tried a high note and the cat, Valachi,
jumped right up from the floor and landed on my bosom.
So now I warm up with a recorder. I breathe through it,
and I play higgledy-piggledy music on it. Every night before bed in the country, I go to the head of the cellar stairs

and play, and Valachi comes bounding up. In addition to
the cat, I always have dogs. Just nondescript dogs that
come and go. I love animals. Deer come within a hundred
feet of the house and stand there with their heads in the air.
And there are foxes and raccoons. I have some neighbors
who had a bunch of raccoons last summer who'd come to
their screen door in the kitchen every evening after dinner
and pry it open and then let it bang. They'd keep doing it
until they were fed with graham crackers and leftovers.
You become aware of so many things in the country that
city people simply don't know about. Like the crickets
chirp-chirp-chirping. To me, they have always sounded
like sleigh bells, and it's a pity there aren't more around at
Christmastime. One autumn evening a while ago, I was
driving by a big field, and it looked totally black, as if some
farmer had burned it off. Then a strip of the black suddenly moved up into the air against the evening sky, formed
into a flock of birds, and flew away after a lead bird. There
was a pause, and a second formation took off, again with a
leader. And so it went, a magic, secret ritual. I sat there fifteen minutes watching, until the field was empty. My house
is surrounded by cow farms, and I love to see the cows
standing on hillsides. I've had the house many years. My
family came from North Wales, and I used to go there for
holidays as a child. I remember endless fields of poppies and
wheat and blue cornflowers and how we'd return from long
walks decked out with bracelets and necklaces of daisies
and buttercups, and I knew that one day I had to have a
place in the country. Of course, I never could have bought
it now. I got it for nothing, and bit by bit through the years,
when I've had a few extra dollars, I've fixed it up. I can't
garden much anymore, so I'd like to have the place planted
with flowering trees—cherry and crabapple and dogwood
and wisteria. Then I'd have a thing of glory. I have a huge
bird population. I buy sunflower seeds by the fifty-pound
bag. The birds take all my pocket money. When I come
down in the morning in winter, they're all sitting and wait-

ing on the telegraph line for me to put out some food, and when I do it's as if they were saying, 'All right, boys. The restaurant is open. Let's go.' "

The car pulled up at the stage door, and Mabel Mercer walked to the greenroom, backstage, where Cavett's guests wait their turn. It was furnished with comfortable chairs, a color television set, and fifty or sixty photographs of Cavett's guests in action on his show. Beard helped Mabel Mercer out of her coat. "There goes my stomach," she said. "I've been in this business nearly sixty years, and I still get butterflies at times like this."

"It's the adrenalin working, Mabel," Beard said. He felt the clothesbag. "Uh-oh! The gowns have fallen down in the bottom!"

Mabel Mercer felt the bag. "No, they haven't, Harry. They're folded over hangers. Those are shoes in the bottom."

"I hope you're right," Beard said.

The stage manager took Mabel Mercer onstage, and she sat down in a large yellow armchair. She ran through the two songs she would do—"Too Long at the Fair," by Billy Barnes, and Lerner and Lane's "Wait 'Til We're Sixty-five." They went well. She was told her black gown would be better, and she went off to a dressing room. Beard ordered tea with honey for her. "It's taken seventy-two hours to prepare her for this," he said. "She's like a child who has to go to the hospital. I finally told her if she wasn't careful she'd be all right. But she's so natural and offhanded-seeming she can't go wrong. Mabel has walked alone. She has never deviated from what she knew had to be done. It has never been a question of money or vogue."

Mabel Mercer reappeared, in a resplendent black gown threaded with silver. She had a red shawl around her shoulders. She sat down and sipped her tea. One of Cavett's assistants told her she would be on first and that Cavett would like to talk with her on camera before she sang. The greenroom was filling up. Robert Theobald, an economic analyst, arrived, and then Shirley Temple Black, in a red dress. She sat down near Mabel Mercer and took out a cigarette. "Do you mind if I smoke?" she asked.

"Of course not, dear," Mabel Mercer replied. "It only bothers me when I'm singing. Years ago, in Paris, when anyone started to smoke a cigar in a place where I was working, he would be asked to put it out, and of course he did. It's not that way anymore." A Cavett assistant asked her if she would like more tea, and she said, "Yes. Sweeten the kitty, if you would."

Cavett came in and shook hands with everyone. He left, and the greenroom settled down to watch her on the television set. After Cavett's monologue, Mabel Mercer went onstage. She looked relaxed and elegant, and she spoke easily and with surprising freeness. She told Cavett that her father, whom she had never known, was an American Negro and that her mother was white. She had been born in Staffordshire, in 1900, into a bohemian household full of painters and people in show business. She said that when she was twelve she told her grandmother, who took care of her while her mother was on the road, that she wanted to be an engineer, and was informed that this was not suitable for young ladies. She was put in a convent boarding school when she was seven, and it was there she realized that there was something different about her. Her schoolmates thought that perhaps she was an African princess, but, if she was, why did she speak English so well? In time, she became a sort of mascot at the school, and was given the nickname Golliwog. She said that the only thing that bothered her was that she had short hair and all the other girls had long plaits, so she tied a couple of pieces of string to a headband and let them hang down like pigtails. Cavett asked her about her years in Paris in the twenties and thirties, and she told him about singing at Bricktop's, and about meeting Cole Porter and Vincent Youmans and Gertrude Stein and Ernest Hemingway. But, she said, none of them made a very deep impression, because they were all young together, all struggling together. There came a commercial, and then Mabel Mercer, seated in the yellow chair, her hands in her lap, her shawl about her shoulders, her composure complete, sang her two songs, with great effect. Her diction was glass, and her voice sure and strong. And she got several good laughs in just the right places in "Wait 'Til We're Sixty-five," a song that has to do with maturing bonds and Social Security, and "Tampa, Fla." She came back to the greenroom, somewhat breathless, and there was a heavy round of applause. A stagehand said Cavett would like her onstage for the rest of the show, and she went back. One of Cavett's assistants said that it was the first time she had ever heard applause in the greenroom.

After Mabel Mercer had changed into her street clothes, she went out through the stage door. It was four o'clock. There was a crowd of autograph seekers on the sidewalk, and she was immediately surrounded. She wrote slowly, but she did sign almost a dozen times. All the while, a huge A.B.C. policeman with a Brendan Behan face and a matching brogue towered over her. He kept saying, "All right, Mabel. You don't have to do so many. . . . One more, Mabel, and I'll take you to the car. . . . Now, that's it. You'll catch your death."

She got into the car. "Well, that's the first time that's happened to me in all these years—all those autographs," she said.

"You're a living legend, Mabel," Beard said.

"Don't say that, Harry," she replied. "It makes me very nervous. Let's have some lunch."

"All right," he said, and told the driver to go to Michael's Pub, on East Fifty-fifth Street. It was nearly empty. Mabel Mercer ordered a Bloody Mary ("I'm going to break my rule and celebrate"), soup, and a spinach salad. "My life has come in three parts—England, France, and America," she said, after she had finished her Bloody Mary. "My mother was short and my stepfather was tall and skinny, and they called their act, which was vaudeville, of course, Ling and Long. I'll never forget one part of it. They'd all put on white tennis clothes and step out on a simulated court and the lights would go down and they'd throw luminous clubs back and forth across the net. My stepfather had invented the luminous clubs, and you'd see these squashy balls of light drifting back and forth through the dark, and it was a beautiful spectacle. In those days, vaudeville was full of jugglers and acrobats and tumblers. The circus is about the only place you find them now. My mother and stepfather had come over to America on tour in 1912 and were stranded by the war, and when I got out of school, in 1914, I went into my aunt's act. It was a family singing-and-dancing act, and I started as a dancer. We went all over England on the vaudeville circuit, and we always travelled on Sundays. We'd hire our own railroad coach, and there would be a sign in the window saying who we were. When we'd get to a new town, there'd be the excitement of seeing old friends and of finding out where you'd be on the bill. The closing act was tops, and I think we made it as the next-to-last act a couple of times. In 1919, another girl and I formed a dancing act and took it to Brussels, and several years later I joined Lew Leslie's 'Black-Birds,' in London, with Florence Mills. After that, I became part of a vocal trio—two men and myself. We sang everything, a cappella and with piano accompaniment—lieder, Negro spirituals, French songs, 'Yes, We Have No Bananas,' 'Carolina in the Morning.' One of the men had been a choirmaster, and it was he who caused me to start studying singing. I studied in Paris and London, and I had aspirations to be a concert singer. But it just didn't work out that way. I paid for my lessons by working in shows and singing in night clubs, and that's no way to become a classical singer. I worked in a variety of shows, travelling all over Europe. One was a circus, where we sang between the acts, and another was *The Chocolate Kiddies*. It played in Vienna and in Cairo and Alexandria. I'd go out to the Pyramids every day. It was when they were excavating the Sphinx, and I remember the workers passing pails of sand along and singing chants, like the American gandy dancers. By the thirties, I had settled pretty much into Bricktop's, and it was a lovely era. Bricktop's was very chic, and money was plentiful.

There were banquettes around the walls, lit from behind, and an orchestra and a small dance floor. I'd sit right at people's tables and sing to them. That sort of intimate singing is tricky, you know. You can't *look* at the people you are singing to. They get embarrassed. So you look at the ceiling or the far corner of the room, and then they can stare at you and know that you won't look down and catch them. Sometimes we'd sing all night, and once I remember stopping in a café on the way home and listening to Louis Armstrong and Django Reinhardt, the gypsy guitarist, playing duets together. They were still there at noon, playing, just the two of them. In 1938, I came over here to work in the Ruban Bleu. It was run by Herbert Jacoby, whom I'd worked for in Paris, and Cy Walter was my accompanist. Then I worked for a while in the Bahamas, where I got to know the Duke and Duchess of Windsor. And in 1941 I went back in the Ruban Bleu and then opened at Tony's, on Fifty-second Street. Billie Holiday was working across the street, and she came in so much that her boss got mad and told her she wasn't being paid to listen to me."

Mabel Mercer had finished her salad, and she looked tired. She said she was going back to the hotel to take a nap. "I don't remember when I last got eight straight hours of sleep. I suppose it's age. I wake up every couple of hours all night and I read or take a hot bath and sometimes that helps."

The St. Regis Room was already full at nine-thirty, and Mabel Mercer, again in her black gown, was seated at a corner table with several priests. At ten minutes of ten, she arranged herself in her chair, a green shawl around her shoulders. A wineglass of hot water with honey and lemon and slices of orange in it sat beside her on the piano. She said something to Jimmy Lyon, gazed serenely over the heads of her listeners, and started George Gershwin's " 'S Wonderful." Bart Howard's "My Love Is a Wanderer" came next, and then another Gershwin, "Isn't It a Pity?" After "Season's Greetings," by Rod Warren, she rearranged her shawl around her waist and tied it loosely. Portia Nelson's "Sunday in New York" and Rodgers and Hart's "Falling in Love with Love" were followed by Cy Coleman's "Sweet Talk." Then came Bob Merrill's "Mira," a song from *Sesame Street* written by Joe Raposo ("Bein' Green"), and Jerome Kern's "Remind Me." The Kern was highlighted by beautifully rolled "r"s. She paused for a moment, and then she gave Cole Porter's "Down in the Depths on the Ninetieth Floor" a beautiful rendition, and ended with the songs she had done on the Cavett show. She bowed her way out of the room, and when she came back she did Cy Coleman and Dorothy Fields' "Baby, Dream Your Dream" as an encore.

She sat down with Harry Beard and the midwestern reporter and ordered tea and honey. Beard said the Cavett show would be on in twenty minutes, and that he wanted to go and find a television set. The reporter asked her how many songs she knows.

"I guess I know roughly a thousand," she answered. "I can sing three or four hundred of them without too much brushing up. I learned a long time ago that you have to keep your mind exactly on what you're doing when you sing. If stray thoughts suddenly pop into your head, you're apt to forget the words. It's happened to me more than once. When it does, I either repeat what I've just sung or sing a line or two of nonsense until the right words come back. They're always there, stored safely away somewhere in the back of my head. I think constantly about the lyrics and what they mean, and I try and make my listeners feel the vision of what the words are saying. All of us know about sorrow and tears and laughter, so it's not my job to sing *my* emotions but to sing my *listeners'* emotions. Then they can take them home with them. In a way, my singing is like putting on certain sets of clothes every night. I'd be a total wreck if I lived all the emotions I sing about. It happened to me just once. I was sitting at a table with some people and singing 'The Last Time I Saw Paris,' and so many things started going through the back of my mind about Brick's and my little apartment in Paris and so forth that I had to stop and excuse myself. At first, I found this sort of intimate singing a terrible wear and tear. I'd get so nervous my lip would tremble and my legs wobble. I'd pray I could walk across the stage and not let it show. I'd sense unfriendly people in the audience or I'd hear a man leave in the middle of a set and say to the maître d., 'Who told *her* she could sing?' Then I understood that you simply cannot please everybody and that there will always be two or three people out front who understand, and it is to *them* that you should sing. I don't know where my sense of diction came from. Perhaps I got it in school. Perhaps it came from my mother. Before she came over here, she'd take me into an empty theatre where she was working, and she'd go up to the top gallery and make me stand down on the stage and sing. I was a very shy child, even with her, but she'd say, 'All right, sing! And I want to understand every word!' I just don't know, I've never had any wish to be famous, and I've always wondered: How can those people sit out there and listen to *me?* If I ever have it to do all over again, I'd like to be a painter, like my grandfather. Or a writer. Something permanent. Look at Mme. Curie. Maybe I'd write children's books about sitting on the beach and the sunbeams coming down and people coming down the beams and talking to me. Fantasies. But I don't suppose I'll ever have the chance."

Coming Out
Again

Anita Ellis

The great dramatic soprano Eileen Farrell considers Anita
Ellis the best American popular singer—praise not from the
mountain for the molehill but from a superb classical singer
who can sing popular music very well for a superb popular
singer who can sing classical music very well. Miss Farrell
has held this opinion for some years, and when she was asked
about it recently she simply said that she knew of no super-
latives that Anita Ellis didn't deserve. Anita Ellis is aware of
Eileen Farrell's admiration, but she has never been able
wholly to accept it. It is only in the past several years that
she has allowed herself even to consider the possibility that
she might have an out-of-the-way vocal instrument, for she
has suffered all her life from acute stagefright. For as long
as she can remember, she has been frightened of performing
(even *en famille*), and she is still frightened. She first realized the extent of her fear in 1951, when the producer
Max Liebman signed her for the *Show of Shows*, with Sid
Caesar and Imogene Coca. "I opened my mouth to sing at

my first rehearsal," she once said, "and nothing came out. Mel Brooks was there, and he kept whispering, 'Relax, Anita, relax,' but it didn't help, and afterward I couldn't even talk." She has reached the point of being able to will herself to perform, but it is far from easy. When, after fifteen years of semi-retirement, she agreed to come out again and sing at Michael's Pub in December, 1974, she would tell her audience between numbers what agony it was for her to be there—her deceptively loose arms ending in tight white fists, her nearsighted gaze focussed blankly in the middle distance. These *cris de cœur* evoked antithetical emotions in her listeners—sympathy because of her obvious anguish, and annoyance because she had breached the magic, transparent wall between performer and audience. But she completed the seven-week engagement, and with such telling effect that she enlarged her already legendary reputation.

Her size and bearing and dress onstage amount to camouflage. She favors dark, diminishing clothes (turtlenecks and pants), and she is no bigger than a coxswain: a shade under five feet two, with a bladelike back and thin, wide shoulders. She keeps her head tilted and her eyes shut—in the hope that when she opens them everybody will be gone. But the fear-quelling momentum she works up for each song makes her a passionate and hypnotic performer, not unlike Judy Garland or Edith Piaf. Her voice is big and surprisingly agile. It is a muscular soprano, capable of endless colors and timbres: pianissimo phrases capped with delicate vibratos; sudden sustained fortissimos that take on a reedy, breathing quality; jubilant middle notes; high clarion tones and low reverential asides. Her dynamics are consummate. Her shouts make us strain to catch the succeeding quiet passage, and her whispers soften her crescendos. Her diction says, These words are important—*listen*. And, caught up immediately by the power and shape of her voice, we are lifted onto the plane she has chosen for the song. When she finishes, her songs don't end; they subside.

In private, she performs constantly and brilliantly. Her speech is an extension of her singing. It is reverse parlando:

speech raised to near-song. She will start a sentence slightly above middle C with a "Well" that stretches out and then slopes into an "I could just tell you," which gives way to a sustained "ah" and the substance of the sentence. Her rhythms and inflections and accents change continually, and form boxy, graceful melodies. She buttresses her talk with her hands and arms and head (she once, in talking of the bateleur eagle of Africa, turned her head abruptly to her left and crooked her arms horizontally to resemble huge partly open wings—and she was the eagle), with bird flutters and akimbos and vigorous nods, and with a dazzling quick smile that opens like a lens.

Anita Ellis lives with her husband, the neurologist Mortimer Shapiro, in an apartment on East End Avenue. The apartment seems to swim from its spacious back kitchen past a couple of dark bedrooms, an equally dark foyer, and a pillared, shadowy living room, and surface at a big picture window that looks out on Carl Schurz Park and the East River. This view consoles her, for she is quick to say, "I don't like New York. It is not my way." Her way is nature, and, in particular, wilderness, and when she looks out it cheers her to "check on the squirrels and the weather and the river and whether there are any new birds in town." She and Shapiro both love wilderness, but they approach it from opposite directions. She is an animal conservationist and he is a big-game hunter. It is not, to her distress, a pastime that he keeps to himself, for their apartment is bedecked from one end to the other with heads and tusks and spears and drums and skins and horns. Al Hirschfeld once likened the living room to the Museum of Natural History— a comparison that delighted the Shapiros, but for different reasons. She had learned to live with this panoply largely by ignoring it, and when they are out in the field (Africa, Alaska, Iran), she sallies off by herself while he hunts. She has great affection for Africa. "I'm home when I'm there," she said, standing in front of the picture window and sipping a glass of clear Japanese tea. "I belong completely. I don't understand what Mort does there—all the killing—even though he says the whole experience fills him with peace. When they go hunting, I go walking. I go down to the water hole at noon and watch the animals gather. They're popularly not supposed to come out in the midday heat, but I know better. The last time we were in Kenya, I found a serene clearing and suddenly there were three elephants. Elephants have miserable eyesight, and they couldn't smell me, because the wind favored me, so they went right by and I could have reached out and touched them. I revere that silence just before sunset, and when the sun suddenly disappears, it's like Toscanini: all the sounds start—birds, insects, and later the hunting animals. Those sounds spread out against the wind. I'm convinced this was where music came from. Man listened to all these creatures and imitated them on flutes and such, and finally wrote the sounds down. The sunsets are sometimes so magnificent they make you want to sing, and I have, for Mort and all the men. I sang in time to it—a lot of blues and made-up songs about what I felt—and I only stopped when the night sounds came up.

"I was in and out of the wilderness all during my child-hood—in the woods near Montreal, where I was born, and out on the Coast, where I grew up. I was born Anita Kert, on April 12, 1920, a seven-month baby and the first of four children. My brother Mortimer was next, and then Evelyn, and finally Larry, and we're all very much alive. Mort is on the management side of the Los Angeles *Times,* and he's a painter and a poet and lives on top of a mountain. Evelyn has been married twice, but hasn't liked it much, and now she's a wine expert. Larry wanted to be a gymnast, and, of course, he's an actor and singer. My father's name is Harry. He was the tenth of thirteen children. His father was Isaac Kert, and he built all the railroads and dams in Canada, and was a great humanist and philanthropist. He came from Kiev when he was fifteen, without a word of English, and became a contractor. He married Jane Cameron, the daughter of a Scottish minister. They lived eventually in what is now La Fontaine Park in Montreal, and they had a hundred and fifty horses. During the summers when my father was growing up, Grandfather Isaac would take the oldest children a thousand miles into the Quebec woods and teach them to hunt and track. He taught me when I was little. Around the turn of the century, one of my father's sisters, Aunt Hattie, begged to go, and Grandpa let her. They found a man with a broken leg out there, and his name was Jack London. Aunt Hattie had green eyes and black hair, and she and London fell in love and had an affair, and my grandfather ended up as a character in a book of his. My father's oldest brother—Sonny, or Maxwell—died in 1908, when my father was thirteen, and the family never recovered. Afterward, they turned totally inward. I have never understood what happened to Maxwell, and I've never been able to find out. He was exceptionally strong and a great shot. But they were remarkable children, and all the rest of them were alive until this year. They only started to go at the age of ninety-eight, and suddenly there are just five left, including my father, who's eighty-three. Grandfather Kert told my father when he was little, 'You are going to be a rabbi,' and from the age of four he had training every afternoon at home. This didn't stop him from becoming an exquisite athlete. He is just five-eight and he's never weighed over a hundred and twenty-eight, but he was a sixty-minute hockey player and a fine boxer. He's perfectly proportioned and so well coördinated it's a pleasure to watch him walk. He married my mother in 1918. She lived in Montreal, but she was born in Bialystok, on the Russian-Polish border, and was brought over during the pogroms when she was four months old. Her parents were Aaron and Molly Peretz—which means 'poet'—but she grew up as Lillian Pearson. She was one of eight, four of whom died in infancy. Her father had had a cement business in Bialystok, but in Montreal he ran a little shop for sailors. He was very orthodox, and eventually he became a holy man and left the running of the store to my grandmother, whom we called Bubba. We'd go to the *shul* with Bubba on Friday night and sit in the balcony and look down at the men, dressed in their yarmulkes and silk talliths and singing their beautiful music. I have tried always to put that music in my singing." She sang eight bars of a Hebrew chant, her voice full and low. She maneuvered the difficult intervals easily, and held the long, flat notes without quavering. "Both Bubba and Zayda, which is what we called Grandfather, lived to be very old. I don't think either pair of grandparents ever saw the other after my mother and father were married."

Anita Ellis had finished her tea and was sitting on a broad sill in front of the picture window. It was a good blue-and-white day—white light and a non-stop blue sky. Carl Schurz Park was almost empty, and trucks moved along Vernon Boulevard, on the other side of the river. A big black-and-green Moran tug passed, going down-stream. She laughed—a fast, bouncing descending run—and said, "Once when I was walking along the river near Forty-ninth Street a tug-boat went by and tied up at a dock, and I asked them if they were going anywhere, and they said the Bronx, and took me along. I had the *best* time. I asked them about sea chanteys—I always ask about music wherever I go. They left me off at Broadway and Two Hundred and Twenty-fifth Street, and gave me a dime to get home on the subway. That sky is what I think of as a California blue. In 1926 or 1927, Grandmother Jane left my grandfather and moved to Hollywood. Two of my aunts were already there, and had told her about the climate and that the place was practically empty. We followed in 1930, and Aunt Ray Champagne—all my aunts married French Catholics—gave us a great big Hupmobile, which had a top that rolled back. My father joined a semi-professional hockey team right away, and for a while that was mainly what we lived on, until he went to work for the LeRoy Diamond Company as a tax man and an accountant. We had the most wonderful life with him. Oh my, I could tell such . . . Well, he took us on the John Muir trail in the Sierra Nevadas, and skin-diving in San Diego. We swam every day, and we learned to sail and ski, both of which I'm still addicted to. We got to know the mountains and the desert, and we got to know the ocean.

My mother—my dear mother, who died in 1978—took care of the other side of our lives, what you might call the domestic and artistic side. She played the piano by ear and sang beautifully. Before she was married, Al Jolson heard her sing and saw her dance at a wedding in Montreal, and for years he tried to get her to take roles in Broadway musicals, but she said no. You didn't sing in public any more than you crossed your legs in public. Even so, she got herself a job singing on the radio once a week in Montreal when I was about one, and when my father found out, he simply updated the taboo—'My wife does not sing on the radio'—and that was that. Mother was dark and had very curly hair. Her eyes were big and brown, and she had Russian cheekbones. She was a quarter of an inch taller than I am, and she had a beautiful figure. I was the ugly duckling of the family, and had slightly crossed eyes until I was fourteen or so. My mother always told me that I wasn't beautiful but that I had a terrific personality. One morning, Mother, who was carrying baby Larry, pulled a Horatio Alger by helping an old man across the street who had a son who was a producer, and soon we were registered at Central Casting. Larry got a baby part right away, and later he and Evelyn were in *Les Misérables*, with Frederic March. I ended up with an M-G-M contract at a hundred and eight dollars a week, and I was in *Babes in Arms*, and *Strike Up the Band*, with Judy Garland and Mickey Rooney. I was literally a born dancer, and I seemed to already know time and double-time steps. Judy and I became quite chummy. We had a language together—fantasy, and all that. She had an exceptional ear, and she never liked to be alone. Mother's ambition all along was for me to be a singer, and when I was sixteen I started studying with Glen Raikes. I graduated from Hollywood High in 1938 and enrolled at U.C.L.A. and I would have been a psychology major except the singing had taken hold, so I switched to the Cincinnati College of Music. I auditioned for Eugene Goossens, and got a scholarship to study opera. I did well in everything—composition, theory—except solfeggio, because I had to perform in class, and that was when my troubles began. In the movies, I had simply been dancing, which was different. You aren't conscious of people staring at you, scrutinizing you, the way they do when you sing. I studied in Cincinnati with Leone Kruse, an old Wagnerian opera star, and she taught me to respect the voice as an instrument, and how the more you do for that instrument the more that instrument will do for you. She taught me that you are limited as a singer only in your range. While I was in Cincinnati, I got a job as a popular singer at WLW, which was the most powerful station in the Midwest. It was a program called *Moon River*, and it was on every midnight. I had already done radio work on the Coast, with Tommy Riggs, the ventriloquist, and had discovered that singing on radio didn't bother me. If there was a studio audience, I'd turn sideways and sing at the control room, which I couldn't see very well anyway, because of my nearsightedness. I stayed in Cincinnati a couple of years, and I met my first husband, Frank Ellis. He was studying drama and he'd gone to the University of Kentucky and he had a beautiful voice. He was Scottish-English-Irish, and tall and handsome. We were married in 1943, and off he went to the Air Force, where he became a colonel. I went home and worked for the Red Cross and got back in U.C.L.A. About this time, I became a friend of Salka Viertel. She had been a famous German actress and was married to the film director Berthold Viertel, who is the principal figure in Christopher Isherwood's *Prater Violet*. Her house was the center of the émigrés on the Coast—the Chaplins, Stravinsky, Schoenberg, Kurt Weill, Huxley, Isherwood, Stephen Spender. Chaplin would tell Salka he wanted So-and-So to dinner, and he'd buy the food and she would cook. One time, I was invited, and I made some remark to Chaplin about how wonderful it was that he had sided with the poor people of the world, how he was one of them. He looked astonished, and he explained that though he had once been poor he had no feeling for the poor, that we would always have poor people no matter what we did, and that he had risen from the poor because he was a genius. I was still at the stage where everything said by father figures like Chaplin was law.

"Then things began to break for me as a singer. I auditioned for William Paley for a fifteen-minute CBS radio program, *Songs Overseas* and got it, over Martha Tilton and I think Peggy Lee and Margaret Whiting. I did it for two years, and then went to New York for my own show on Mutual. Tommy Rockwell, who handled Dinah Shore and Frank Sinatra and Perry Como, took me over, and he wanted to team me up with Como on the show that sent him on his way. But Colonel Ellis came back from overseas and said we were going to the Jackson Army Air Base, in Mississippi, where he was to be a commanding officer. How could I not go, when we'd spent only two weeks together since we'd been married? Tommy Rockwell did everything to talk me out of it, but I went, and it wasn't hard for me. I got into things I'd never imagined—signing up Louis Armstrong and Duke Ellington for dances on the base, organizing lectures for the officers' wives, starting a newspaper, interviewing P.O.W.s. I also began to learn what the real world was like. I discovered the unbelievable life most blacks lead in the South, and I finally got so upset I went to see the governor. He got sore and told me he'd have Frank and me transferred, and the next thing General Curtis LeMay came for a visit and said he'd had complaints. I kept my sanity by learning to fly. When I got my license, Frank and I would go up in a P-38. We'd go up in the sky to play. But pretty soon Frank was relieved and sent to El Paso. El Paso! That did it. I told Frank I was going to resume my singing career. I went back to the Coast, and in 1946 Frank and I were divorced. We were always good friends. He was killed in a plane crash in 1957."

Anita Ellis said it was time to leave for an appointment with Marion Manderen, her voice teacher, who lives in North Tarrytown. Anita was wearing a black turtleneck and black pants. In the cab to Grand Central, she talked with great animation of a trip to China she had taken in the fall of 1976 with her husband and ten economists, doctors, and educators. She found a window seat on the train, and took off her coat. "I've never stopped vocalizing," she said. "It's like meditation for me. It makes me whole and peaceful. My mother and my grandmothers had the most influence on me as a singer. Mother sang Romberg and Kern and Gershwin, and Grandma Jane sang Scottish airs, and Bubba sang Jewish and Russian songs. My sister Evelyn has a beautiful coloratura soprano. I also listened to Jolson and Crosby and Sinatra when I was growing up, and to Mel Tormé and Peggy Lee and Margaret Whiting and Jo Stafford. I didn't hear Billie Holiday at all until I did a benefit with her and Duke Ellington and Ivie Anderson in L.A. I couldn't get over how she changed—from that naked, smoking, tough woman in the dressing room to the cool, motionless, vessel-of-life singer onstage. Ivie Anderson was like a little girl in comparison. It didn't take me long in Cincinnati to find out that emotionally I couldn't be an opera singer. I thought of lieder for a while, and when I sing Sondheim and Wilder and Kern, who often write a form of lieder, I approach their songs that way. I always have to have a subtext, a motivation, before I sing a song. I've used my trips to the wilderness I don't know how many times. Sondheim's 'Anyone Can Whistle' is motivated by a big male zebra in Africa. Our guide had told Morty to try for it. Morty fired and it went down and got up and kept going, and they followed it as it fell and got up, fell and got up, and I ended up behind a tree practically having a nervous breakdown. The words 'I can dance the tango' in 'Anyone' mean we're wildly alive and then they try to kill us when we're doing the best we can. That's what that song is about to me. The subtext of 'I Loves You Porgy' is different but related. In the early fifties, I did a weekend at a hotel on Virginia Beach. The first morning, I was having breakfast looking out over the ocean, and a little child of three or four asked the black woman who was waiting on my table if he could go swimming. Well, what he said in his little voice was 'Fimmin'? Fimmin'?' She told him no, he couldn't swim at that beach, and she'd take him to a water hole later. After breakfast, I found that creature and took him down to the water, and the woman came running, and she was furious. She said, 'You can't do that! You can't do that here! You might get him killed later when he gets bigger and they find out he went swimming at this beach.' When I sing 'I Loves You Porgy,' I'm holding that child by the hand. I'm singing to him, and we're looking for a place we can just be. So my feelings come first, and the words come after and express them on different levels. I have to be careful, though. If I get too involved, I'm afraid I'll wander from the melody. You can't let too much emotion in."

Marion Manderen met the train and drove Anita Ellis a quarter of a mile to her house, which is on a tidal pond near the Hudson. Anita Ellis made a cup of tea to warm her pipes, and Marion Manderen sat down at her piano at one end of her living room. Anita Ellis kicked off her shoes and, standing by the piano in her stocking feet, sipped her tea.

"Marion," she said, "I was thinking on the way up of 1964, when I had the tonsil operation. Do you remember? I couldn't sing a note for six months. Why couldn't I get a note?"

"Your cords weren't coming together," Marion Manderen said. "You couldn't make a singing tone. We worked at least six months. We'd get so absorbed that darkness would fall. Then one day it came. Anita, what I'd like to do first is some humming. I want you to hum until you feel your lip tickle. Do: *me me me may ma moo.*" She sounded middle C several times.

Anita Ellis straightened her back, clasped her hands in front of her, made a triangle with her legs, and looked into the middle distance—or, in this case, into a mirror hanging over a fireplace. She sang the syllables on C as half notes.

"Keep the humming going through it," Marion Manderen said. She sat with her left shoulder to the keyboard, and she mimicked Anita Ellis's mouth motions. "Make it even lighter. Don't press down on the vowels." Marion Manderen moved down two notes. "Make the tones higher in your head, and farther forward. Don't let the energy of your breath lessen. I want it all in one breath." She moved down the keyboard slowly, and stopped at the C below middle C. Anita Ellis was having more trouble the lower she went, and she stopped and laughed.

"I want you to do: *hung me ma may moo*. On the *hung* get right into the vowel, and use the *ng* to resonate. Do it a little faster now. Throw your *hung* out."

Anita Ellis went through the sounds twice. Marion Manderen asked if she was resonating yet, and she said no. Marion Manderen stared at Anita Ellis's mouth as if she could see the tones emerge and were waiting to correct their shape. The two descended an octave and stopped.

Anita Ellis made a face at herself in the mirror. She patted her hair, which was in loose, even curls around her head, and she tweaked her face. "God. I look awful. I better go off to a spa and get refurbished." She laughed and took a sip of tea.

Marion Manderen played an ascending five-note figure. "Let's do: *eeyo eeyo eeyo eeyo eeyo*. I want you to feel it in your cheekbones." Anita Ellis tried the tones twice. "Don't press," Marion Manderen said. "And I want more on the descending line. More, more, more. Keep your throat open, and as you come down let your jaws go."

Anita Ellis's voice had gotten stronger and stronger. Her middle tones boomed a little, and her lower tones weren't scratchy. A half hour had gone by, and during the next ten minutes she worked through a variety of vowels, and rested. Then Marion Manderen said she wanted arpeggios, and Anita Ellis began with the sound *b*, ascended with *ee ee ee ya ya ya*, and descended with four *a* sounds.

"Keep your upper jaw more elevated, Anita. As you come down, you like to make that gutsy sound. But at the same time keep that *aaa* going out. Keep thinking *aaa* on each note. We want to keep that Italian sound. I have an image of a croquet wicket, of an arch of sounds."

"I think of a dolphin," Anita Ellis said.

"Slide down, slide down. If you can, slide on the outermost rim of that arc without pressing."

A couple of double arpeggios followed, and then a cluster of staccato-note exercises, and the lesson ended with more arpeggios. Anita Ellis's voice had grown strong and pure and open. "All right, Anita," Marion Manderen said on the last run-through. "Crescendo that last note. It's a focussed note, and I want a wide sound, which is the hardest to crescendo. I want energy. I want you to resonate. There! You did it!" Marion Manderen stood up and laughed and clapped her hands once. She headed toward her kitchen. "Before you go, I have some basil from my garden to give you."

The sun, hanging over the Palisades, rode with the train, and its water-reflected light shimmied on the ceiling of the car. Anita Ellis's small, neat profile was dark and sharp against the window. She was quiet for a time, and then she said, "I plunged into work after Frank and I were divorced. I did Red Skelton and Jack Carson, and I had my own show. Then Columbia gave me a contract to dub some Rita Hayworth pictures—*Gilda* and *Down to Earth* and *Loves of Carmen* and *Lady from Shanghai*. Orson Welles directed *Lady*, and he was always having vituperative fits. If anybody said they were tired, he'd shout, 'Why do you have to sleep? You don't sleep when you work! You work and work and work, and when the picture is finished you sleep!' I made lots and lots of money and bought a big house in the Hollywood Hills for my father and mother. Everybody had a room and a bath, and we were one big happy family again. Larry and Evelyn were there, too. We had always gotten along very well. We had never felt the need for anyone else. When Grandma Jane was alive, we had Sunday-night dinner at her house, and the whole family came—in Montreal and later on the Coast. We sang and did Highland flings and Russian kozachoks. It was a *freilich*, a happy time. I hung out, too, with Saul and Ethel Chaplin. They had a kind of musical salon, and you'd see Judy Holliday, and Comden and Green, and Gene Kelly, and Nora Kaye, and Shelley Winters. The songwriters came and ran down their new songs. I got to know Arthur Laurents there, and we became bosom friends and gave little dinners for screenwriters and the Hollywood Ten and such.

"In 1949, I went to Paris for two and a half months to make some recordings, and I thrived. I met Art Buchwald at a money changer's in the old Jewish section. He'd written a play that nobody in the States would read, so he'd gone to Paris on the G.I. Bill and was a student at the Alliance Française. He was a very funny man. I also met Harry Kurnitz, the screenwriter, at the money changer's, and one night Kurnitz, who had lots of money, took Buchwald and me to dinner at an incredibly plush French-Russian restaurant. I had had almost nothing to drink in my life, but that night I had a lot of champagne and got excited and festive, in my Bernardo sandals and my red silk dress with its pleated skirt. Kurnitz cried and cried and kept asking the musicians in the restaurant to play sad Jewish songs, and Buchwald and I laughed and laughed, and finally I got sick and had to be taken home. I also got to know Maxim De Beix, who was with *Variety* and was quite old and was married to a young, pretty woman who worked in a *parfumerie*. When he took me to lunch once, I asked if I could bring Art, because I knew Art wanted somehow to get a job on the Paris *Tribune*. At lunch, De Beix said that he was going to die soon and that when he did Art could take his place with *Variety*. Well, I tell you . . . he looked marvellous and we all laughed, but do you know he *did* die soon and Art *did* take his place, and from there worked his way to the *Trib*.

"When I got back, I went to Hollywood and dubbed for Vera-Ellen in *Three Little Words* and *The Belle of New York*. Fred Astaire was in both of them, and I had to sound like her and phrase like him—not a breath apart. He was a relentless perfectionist. He worked days on a single step. He was interested in the lighting and where the shadows fell. He was interested in how the colors of the sets jibed with the songs and with his dances. Everything had to mesh before you could shoot a foot of film. While I was out there, I went to a party at Danny Kaye's, and Johnny Green *made* me sing 'All the Things You Are' against my every wish, and that was when Max Liebman heard me. After the disaster at the rehearsal, I went to an analyst in New York and at the same time worked with Luther Henderson, the pianist and composer. After six months, the analyst said that if we were to continue, I'd have to get a singing job. I auditioned, and followed Pearl Bailey into La Vie en Rose. I was so scared opening night I broke out in blotches and had to sing the verse of my first song behind the curtain before my brother Larry pushed me onto the stage. Herbert Jacoby and Max Gordon heard me, and I went back and forth between the Angel and the Village Vanguard for the next couple of years, and then into Bon Soir. I stayed with the analyst four or five days a week for three years, but I still had a long way to go. I could have made a lot of money, but my fear made me turn down jobs all over the place. I did understudy Pat Suzuki and Arabella Hong in *Flower Drum Song*, but only because Oscar Hammerstein wanted me to. It was the last big job I took until I went into Michael's Pub.

"On July 31, 1960, I married Mort Shapiro. I'd met him in the fifties, when his first wife was still alive, and I knew I was hooked and tried for years to get over it. Mort doesn't talk about his past much, but things have filtered through, such as his father's having started out as a ragpicker on the Lower East Side and having become extremely wealthy in the cloth business; Mort's being brought up with a silver spoon and going to Columbia when he was fifteen; his father's disinheriting him because Mort's first wife was much older than he was. We were married in an empty room in a house in Turtle Bay that Stephen Sondheim had just bought. He lived on the bottom two floors, and we moved into the top three. I loved being married, and I became a *wife.* I knew almost nothing about cooking, so I read *Larousse Gastronomique*, which lets you go at your own pace, and I took five lessons from Dione Lucas. Now I'm a very good cook. Food has the most beautiful textures and colors and smells, and I love the peace and contentment of preparing it and the pleasure of giving it away. Right after we were married, though, Mort said that we had to have Billy Rose for dinner, and we did, along with Harold Rome and Melanie Kahane. We used to go to Chambord for dinner and I knew the maître d', so I went to him and told him how many we were having, and he fixed duck with olives and cold mussels in lemon sauce. I carried the whole works home myself and fixed some rice and everyone sat on boxes around the table and said they'd never tasted such a meal. I didn't tell Mort what I'd done for years. I had gotten to know a lot of the painters—Stephen Greene and Helen Frankenthaler and Andy Warhol, when he was just starting —and they began coming to dinner, and sometimes a hundred people would eat my paella and mussels in wine. Jasper Johns and Larry Rivers and Frank Stella would come, and Ellis Larkins would play, and sometimes I'd sing. Virgil Thomson also came, and he still does. He loves to talk, and the more shocking he is the better he likes it."

Anita Ellis took a cab from Grand Central to East End Avenue, and it went up Madison Avenue in the yellow evening light. "I never thought to ask for things for myself before," she said, "but maybe I'll sing more now and be less of a housewife. I'm scheduled for a concert at Alice Tully, and Ellis Larkins and I have just made a record. I think I know now that I can sing well."